Designing for XOOPS

Designing for XOOPS

Sun Ruoyu

O'REILLY®

Beijing · Cambridge · Farnham · Köln · Sebastopol · Tokyo

Designing for XOOPS

by Sun Ruoyu

Published by O'Reilly Media, Inc., 1005 Gravenstein Highway North, Sebastopol, CA 95472.

O'Reilly books may be purchased for educational, business, or sales promotional use. Online editions are also available for most titles (*http://my.safaribooksonline.com*). For more information, contact our corporate/institutional sales department: (800) 998-9938 or *corporate@oreilly.com*.

Editor: Julie Steele	**Cover Designer:** Karen Montgomery
Production Editor: Kristen Borg	**Interior Designer:** David Futato
Proofreader: O'Reilly Production Services	**Illustrator:** Robert Romano

Printing History:

July 2011:	First Edition.

ISBN: 978-1-449-30896-4

[LSI]

1310563069

Table of Contents

Preface

What Is XOOPS?

Before you dive into this book, I would like to first extend my warm welcome to you as you enter the world of XOOPS. XOOPS is an acronym of e**X**tensible **O**bject **O**riented **P**ortal **S**ystem. It is an open-source application platform and Content Management System (CMS) written in PHP. It is built for developing a variety of solutions in a modular fashion, for both small and large interactive dynamic community websites, company portals, intranets, weblogs, and much more. By installing different modules, you can build quite different websites.

XOOPS is released under the terms of the GNU General Public License (GPL) and is free to use and modify. It is also free to redistribute as long as you abide by the distribution terms of the GPL.

Why Use XOOPS?

XOOPS is shipped with a nice installer and can be easily deployed on a web-hosted server. In XOOPS 2.5, a more user-friendly backend administration has been introduced. This makes managing a complex website very easy and intuitive. You need almost no programming knowledge to build a website!

Due to the very flexible architecture of XOOPS, a developer (or even an advanced user), can create a vast variety of applications on top of XOOPS, including diaries, team rankings for sporting events, school administration systems, photo galleries, newspapers/magazines, and sophisticated ecommerce packages.

Powerful Modules

The most common application for XOOPS is as a CMS. With powerful modules contributed by developers all over the world, you can create and manage content easily.

Themes and Templates

XOOPS uses Smarty—one of the most popular template engines in PHP—as its template engine. This makes it easier for designers to get used to the syntax. You don't have to deal with raw PHP code.

In addition, XOOPS is equipped with a lot of Smarty plug-ins to make life easier for designers.

User Management

XOOPS has a robust user management system. This is a key feature for applications like community websites. Users can search for other users by various criteria, or send email and private messages to other users through a template-based messaging system. And there are "social network" modules for XOOPS that can help enhance user interaction. XOOPS also has a powerful and user-friendly permissions system, which enables administrators to set permissions by group.

Supported Worldwide

XOOPS was created and is maintained by a team of several hard-working volunteers located all over the world. The XOOPS community has more than a dozen official support sites around the world for non-English-speaking users. XOOPS fully supports multi-byte languages, including Japanese, Simplified and Traditional Chinese, Korean, and so on.

If you have any questions, the community can always help you. And as you become an expert on XOOPS, please join the community and make your own contribution!

Brief History of XOOPS

The roots of XOOPS go back to PHPNuke, which was created by Francisco Burzi in 2000. As it sometimes happens within open source projects, a few of the developers who worked on PHPNuke decided to create something closer to their vision for a CMS, which they felt should be written with Object Oriented Programming (OOP) principles and technology. The result of their work became what we know today as XOOPS.

Over its 10 years of existence, XOOPS has reinvented itself many times. Besides being one of the OOP pioneers in the CMS area, it was also one of the first to add the Smarty templating system. Although Smarty is somewhat controversial, no one can deny that using it is much easier than using raw PHP code to create themes. In addition, we can take advantage of different Smarty plug-ins to enhance its flexibility.

Now XOOPS is evolving again. This time, it has been rewritten from scratch using the Zend Framework. While currently in Alpha release, the new version's release is planned for the end of 2011.

What This Book Covers

This book covers the whole workflow of building a XOOPS theme from scratch.

Chapter 1, Before the Journey, generally describes the workflow and introduces the basic concepts that you need to know. It briefly covers how to set up Apache, PHP, and MySQL environments for XOOPS. I'll also talk about what tools you need to build a theme.

Chapter 2, Elements of a XOOPS Theme, starts by introducing the plain framework for themes. Although you can build your theme from a blank XHTML file, it simply takes too much time and requires a lot of thinking. By using the simplest theme framework, I will introduce the template engine structures of XOOPS.

Chapter 3, Converting an Existing XHTML Template, mainly introduces how to apply an existing XHTML template to XOOPS. This will give you a more thorough look at the template engine.

Chapter 4, Styling XOOPS and Creating a Theme from 960, introduces more details on CSS styling. It will also illustrate how to create a XOOPS theme using 960 Framework for XOOPS, and how to make use of the theme framework to save time and code.

Chapter 5, jQuery and UI Libraries for XOOPS Themes, briefly discusses how to add jQuery and jQuery-based UI libraries to the theme to achieve complex effects. Two detailed case studies will help give you a deeper understanding of this subject.

Chapter 6, Module Template Override, covers the module template override. This allows you to control the template of each individual module by your XOOPS theme. jQuery integrations will also be discussed in this chapter

Chapter 7, Block Anywhere Techniques, mainly discusses "block anywhere" techniques.

Chapter 8, Case Study: My TinyMag, will summarize all you've learned in previous chapters in a case study: we'll go from an idea to a complete website.

To take it to the next level, see the materials available on the book's support site at *http://insraq.me/book/*. If you have the ebook, you were also given a file named *cny_sale_package.zip* that contains premium themes (which I hope will help your studies), free to those who purchase this book. If you purchased a hard copy, you can get these themes by going to *http://insraq.me/book/*—follow the instructions there and use the coupon code DFXT11.

What You Need to Know

This is a designer's guide. So I assume that you know XHTML and CSS quite well.

A little prior knowledge of XOOPS is very helpful. You should at least know how to *install* XOOPS and conduct basic operations. And your knowledge of other CMSes might also help you.

There are also some things you don't need to know:

- PHP know-how is not necessary. In fact, I will not talk about PHP at all. Many great PHP programmers develop XOOPS to save designers from the dealing with PHP code.

- In-depth JavaScript knowledge is not required, though a basic understanding of JavaScript is quite useful. This book focuses on jQuery, a JavaScript Library that allows designers to write less and do more. It is much easier than the traditional JavaScript approach.

- Unix/Linux server-related knowledge is not needed (though it is recommended for webmasters). This book focuses on the designing process. In fact, the main operating system used here is Windows. Server-related configuration is not covered.

Who Is This Book For?

If you fall into any of these categories, this book is for you:

- You are running a XOOPS website and have some basic understanding of the framework. Now you want to customize the look of your website. This book includes in-depth discussions on designing techniques and tricks.

- You have planned several other websites powered by XOOPS, but you want to improve your design skills with regard to XOOPS. You will definitely benefit from the comprehensive coverage of XOOPS design, especially the last case study, which explains how to turn an idea into a full-featured website.

- You are a designer and new to XOOPS, and you want to design for XOOPS to extend your career opportunities. This book makes several comparisons between (X)HTML template and the XOOPS theme engine. There is also a tutorial on how to port an existing (X)HTML template to XOOPS in Chapter 3.

For absolute beginners, I will not go through the basic concepts here. But XOOPS is quite easy to use, especially the latest version, 2.5, which has a very intuitive backend. And you can always get help from the XOOPS community at www.xoops.org (*http://www.xoops.org*). After you have some basic knowledge of XOOPS, this book will quickly deepen your understanding of XOOPS themes and templates.

Conventions Used in This Book

The following typographical conventions are used in this book:

Italic

    Indicates file names, directories, new terms, URLs, clickable items in the interface such as menu items and buttons, and emphasized text.

`Constant width`

Used for program listings, as well as within paragraphs to refer to program elements such as variable or function names, databases, data types, environment variables, statements, and keywords.

`Constant width bold`

Shows commands or other text that should be typed literally by the user, as well as the filename at the beginning of a code example.

`Constant width italic`

Shows text that should be replaced with user-supplied values or by values determined by context.

 This icon signifies a tip, suggestion, or general note.

 This icon indicates a warning or caution.

Path and Folders

XOOPS represents your XOOPS root path. Therefore, *XOOPS* may translate to *C: \XAMPP\htdocs\XOOPS* on your computer.

XOOPS/themes means the *themes* folder in your XOOPS root. You might notice that Windows uses the backslash (\)—but I will use slash (/), which is the convention in Linux.

Using Code Examples

This book is here to help you get your job done. In general, you may use the code in this book in your programs and documentation. You do not need to contact us for permission unless you're reproducing a significant portion of the code. For example, writing a program that uses several chunks of code from this book does not require permission. Selling or distributing a CD-ROM of examples from O'Reilly books does require permission. Answering a question by citing this book and quoting example code does not require permission. Incorporating a significant amount of example code from this book into your product's documentation does require permission.

We appreciate, but do not require, attribution. An attribution usually includes the title, author, publisher, and ISBN. For example: "*Designing for XOOPS* by Sun Ruoyu. Copyright 2011 XOOPS Foundation, 978-1-449-30896-4."

If you feel your use of code examples falls outside fair use or the permission given above, feel free to contact us at *permissions@oreilly.com*.

We'd Like to Hear from You

Please address comments and questions concerning this book to the publisher:

O'Reilly Media, Inc.
1005 Gravenstein Highway North
Sebastopol, CA 95472
(800) 998-9938 (in the United States or Canada)
(707) 829-0515 (international or local)
(707) 829-0104 (fax)

We have a web page for this book, where we list errata, examples, and any additional information. You can access this page at:

http://oreilly.com/catalog/9781449308964/

To comment or ask technical questions about this book, send email to:

bookquestions@oreilly.com

For more information about our books, courses, conferences, and news, see our website at *http://www.oreilly.com*.

Find us on Facebook: *http://facebook.com/oreilly*

Follow us on Twitter: *http://twitter.com/oreillymedia*

Watch us on YouTube: *http://www.youtube.com/oreillymedia*

Safari® Books Online

Safari Books Online is an on-demand digital library that lets you easily search over 7,500 technology and creative reference books and videos to find the answers you need quickly.

With a subscription, you can read any page and watch any video from our library online. Read books on your cell phone and mobile devices. Access new titles before they are available for print, and get exclusive access to manuscripts in development and post feedback for the authors. Copy and paste code samples, organize your favorites, download chapters, bookmark key sections, create notes, print out pages, and benefit from tons of other time-saving features.

O'Reilly Media has uploaded this book to the Safari Books Online service. To have full digital access to this book and others on similar topics from O'Reilly and other publishers, sign up for free at *http://my.safaribooksonline.com*.

Acknowledgments

First, I have to thank the core developers of XOOPS—without them, I could not have written this book. Also thanks to the many module developers whose modules I made use of while putting together this book.

Publishing the book is not easier than writing it; I got a lot of help from the community. I want to especially thank Michael (*Mamba*), who helped me deal with the publishing world. Mirza (*Bleekk*) reviewed the technical details of the book, and provided a lot of useful feedback. The editor of this book, Julie Steele; production editor Kristen Borg; and the whole O'Reilly team have done a wonderful job during the publishing process.

Finally, I want to thank my friends and family, who have always been supporting me and made this happen.

CHAPTER 1

Before the Journey

Prepare the Tools

There is an old Chinese saying: "To do a good job, one must first sharpen one's tools." So before you start designing a XOOPS theme, you must first get yourself (and your computer) prepared.

I'll first describe the general workflow and list what tools you will need for each step.

General Workflow of Designing a XOOPS Theme

Step 1: Create a Web Design

As a designer, you are of course familiar with this procedure. Whether you start with pencil and paper or Photoshop is up to you. As long as your final output is (X)HTML and CSS, it will be fine.

Step 2: Convert the XHTML template to a XOOPS theme

In this step, you will need a copy of XOOPS installed on your computer. XOOPS requires PHP and MySQL, so you should first set up the environment. There are plenty of ways to do this, but the most simple way is to use *XAMPP*.

First, go to *http://www.apachefriends.org/en/xampp.html*. You can choose the appropriate version according to your operating system. For the illustration in Figure 1-1, I used Windows. I recommend you download the Lite version.

After you get the file, extract it or let it self-extract. Then, enter the folder where you extracted XAMPP Lite, and you will see *xampp-control.exe*, as shown in Figure 1-2.

XAMPP Lite		
Version	Size	Content
XAMPP Lite 1.7.3		Apache 2.2.14 (IPv6 enabled), MySQL 5.1.41 + PBXT engine, PHP 5.3.1, OpenSSL 0.9.8l, phpMyAdmin 3.2.4, XAMPP Control Panel 2.5.8, XAMPP CLI Bundle 1.6, Webalizer 2.21-02, msmtp 1.4.19, SQLite 2.8.17, SQLite 3.6.20, Ming 0.4.3 For Windows 2000, XP, Vista, 7. See ⌁ README
⌁ EXE	28 MB	Self-extracting RAR archiv MD5 checksum: ce02838d8e92407926429e3829d113a5
⌁ ZIP	61 MB	ZIP archiv MD5 checksum: af1dfef84d1f14be81b772ca885cb7af

Figure 1-1. This is the Windows distribution of XAMPP Lite I downloaded

⌁ xampp_stop.exe	2009/8/6 0:00	Application	88 KB
xampp-changes.txt	2009/8/6 0:00	Text Document	6 KB
⌁ xampp-control.exe	2009/8/6 0:00	Application	140 KB
⌁ xampp-portcheck.exe	2009/8/6 0:00	Application	161 KB

Figure 1-2. The executable file appears in the extracted folder

Double-click to open it, and you will see an interface similar to that shown in Figure 1-3.

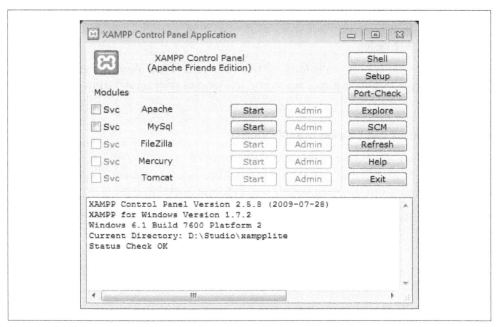

Figure 1-3. The XAMPP Lite interface for Windows

Click the *Start* button next to Apache and MySQL.

When you see the *Running* label next to Apache and MySQL, you have successfully set up the AMP (Apache + MySQL + PHP) environment on your computer.

The next thing to do is to install a copy of XOOPS. It is quite easy, as XOOPS has a very user-friendly installer. Download the archive, extract it, set up the database, run the installer and you're done! There are many tutorials on how to do that, so I'm not going to go into details here.

Step 3: Testing and debugging

You might encounter various problems when you code your theme. Some of them may relate to the template itself—for example, you may make a mistake in the CSS code of the template. Others may be caused by an incorrect implementation of XOOPS template engine. You should make sure that the first type of bugs is fully eliminated before you implement the XOOPS template engine. Otherwise, it will take you twice the time to debug: you will have to consider the bugs in both the original template and the XOOPS template engine implementation.

XOOPS will not turn on the debug option by default. You need to turn it on and select an appropriate method for different purposes (*System Options→Preferences→General Settings*). See Figure 1-4.

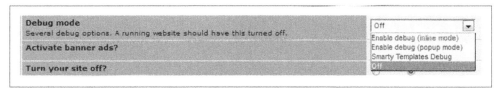

Figure 1-4. Turn on debug mode manually, since the XOOPS default leaves it off

For CSS debugging, I recommend two tools, and they are both add-ons for Firefox: Web Developer Toolbar and Firebug (Figure 1-5).

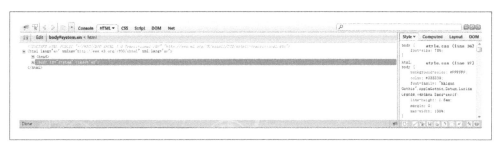

Figure 1-5. The Web Developer Toolbar and Firebug add-ons for Firefox are helpful debugging tools

As a designer, you have probably already installed copies of major browsers so you can debug cross-browser-wise. But if not, you should do that now, too.

CHAPTER 2

Elements of a XOOPS Theme

Now we can really start our journey. It may not be an easy road, but don't worry—I'll be your guide.

Necessary Elements of a XOOPS Theme

Please go to the *XOOPS/theme/default* directory; this holds the default theme of XOOPS. There you can see lots of CSS, HTML, and graphics files, as shown in Figure 2-1.

Are all those files necessary? Of course not. The simplest XOOPS theme needs only one file: *theme.html*. And since you are not in prehistoric times, you should use CSS to control the style instead of directly controlling it in HTML. You can use *theme.html* and *style.css* to build your theme. In the beginning, we will be dealing with these two files pretty much all the time.

Now go to *XOOPS/theme/*, create a new folder, and name it whatever you'd like. I'll use *firsttheme*.

Now let me explain how it works. If we choose to use *firsttheme* as our theme, XOOPS will display *theme.html* under the *firsttheme* folder, no matter what's in that file. Suppose that you write a static HTML file, name it *theme.html* and put it in *firsttheme*. XOOPS will display that HTML file.

Then why bother with XOOPS? You could display that file by double-clicking it. It will not make much difference.

What you are going to do is add some markup that can be read by the XOOPS theme engine. The engine can read your instructions and actually control the way XOOPS displays your website. That's basically the mechanism of the XOOPS theme engine, and is pretty easy to understand.

The next question is how to make use of the "special markup." Instead of introducing these options one by one, I will first give you an example and then explain the markup in it.

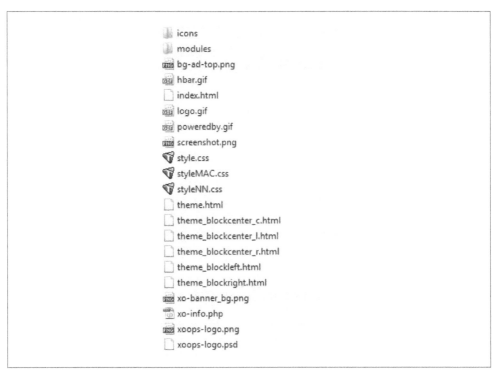

Figure 2-1. The default theme directory in XOOPS contains CSS, HTML, and graphics files

A Simple Example

Erol Konik (known in the forums as *aph3x*) provides a plain XOOPS theme in the XOOPS forum (*http://goo.gl/qXkgv*). It is a very good theme to start with:

```
theme.html
<!DOCTYPE html PUBLIC "-//W3C//DTD XHTML 1.0 Transitional//EN"
    "http://www.w3.org/TR/xhtml1/DTD/xhtml1-transitional.dtd">
<html xmlns="http://www.w3.org/1999/xhtml" xml:lang="<{$xoops_langcode}>"
    lang="<{$xoops_langcode}>">
<head>
<meta http-equiv="content-type" content="text/html; charset=<{$xoops_charset}>" />
<meta http-equiv="content-language" content="<{$xoops_langcode}>" />
<meta name="robots" content="<{$xoops_meta_robots}>" />
<meta name="keywords" content="<{$xoops_meta_keywords}>" />
<meta name="description" content="<{$xoops_meta_description}>" />
<meta name="rating" content="<{$xoops_meta_rating}>" />
<meta name="author" content="<{$xoops_meta_author}>" />
<meta name="copyright" content="<{$xoops_meta_copyright}>" />
<meta name="generator" content="XOOPS" />
<title><{$xoops_sitename}> - <{$xoops_pagetitle}></title>
<link href="<{$xoops_url favicon.ico}>" rel="SHORTCUT ICON" />
<link rel="stylesheet" type="text/css" media="screen"
    href="<{$xoops_url xoops.css }>" />
<link rel="stylesheet" type="text/css" media="screen" href="<{$xoops_themecss}>" />
```

```
<{$xoops_module_header}>
</head>
<body>

<!-- LEFT -->
<{foreach item=block from=$xoBlocks.canvas_left }>
    <{$block.title}>
    <{$block.content}>
<{/foreach}>

<!-- CENTER -->
<{foreach item=block from=$xoBlocks.page_topcenter }>
    <{$block.title}>
    <{$block.content}>
<{/foreach}>

<!-- CENTER LEFT -->
<{foreach item=block from=$xoBlocks.page_topleft }>
    <{$block.title}>
    <{$block.content}>
<{/foreach}>

<!-- CENTER RIGHT -->
<{foreach item=block from=$xoBlocks.page_topright }>
    <{$block.title}>
    <{$block.content}>
<{/foreach}>

<!-- CONTENT PAGES -->
<{$xoops_contents}>

<!-- BOTTOM CENTER -->
<{foreach item=block from=$xoBlocks.page_bottomcenter}>
    <{$block.title}>
    <{$block.content}>
<{/foreach}>

<!-- BOTTOM CENTER LEFT -->
<{foreach item=block from=$xoBlocks.page_bottomleft}>
    <{$block.title}>
    <{$block.content}>
<{/foreach}>

<!-- BOTTOM CENTER RIGHT -->
<{foreach item=block from=$xoBlocks.page_bottomright}>
    <{$block.title}>
    <{$block.content}>
<{/foreach}>

<!-- RIGHT -->
<{foreach item=block from=$xoBlocks.page_right }>
    <{$block.title}>
    <{$block.content}>
<{/foreach}>
```

```
<!-- FOOTER -->
<{$xoops_footer}>
</body>
</html>
```

Block-Displaying Structures

Let's ignore the <head> part for now and focus on <body>. You will find out that there are lots of similar structures:

```
<{foreach item=block from=$*}>
    <{$block.title}>
    <{$block.content}>
<{/foreach}>
```

These are used to display XOOPS blocks. The part between <{foreach}> will be re-peatedly displayed. What does that mean? Well, for example, if you've set the block manager in the XOOPS backend to display four left blocks, then the following section in *theme.html* will be interpreted by XOOPS:

```
theme.html (excerpt)
<{foreach item=block from=$xoBlocks.canvas_left}>
    <{$block.title}>
    <{$block.content}>
<{/foreach}>
```

The output result will be as shown in Figure 2-2.

By using this code in *theme.html*, you are actually telling XOOPS, "OK, please display all the left blocks here, and don't forget to follow the pattern I defined within the <foreach> tag!"

How does XOOPS know whether you are talking about left blocks or not? The key is in the first line:

```
<{foreach item=block from=$xoBlocks.canvas_left}>
```

from=$xoBlocks.canvas_left actually instructs XOOPS to show left blocks only. If you understand this, then you can understand all other similar structures in the code. They are only different in block types.

You can read the comment to see what part the code is actually displaying.

There are eight positions (or places) of blocks in the latest XOOPS, version 2.4. You can match the code with the settings in the XOOPS backend (see Figure 2-3).

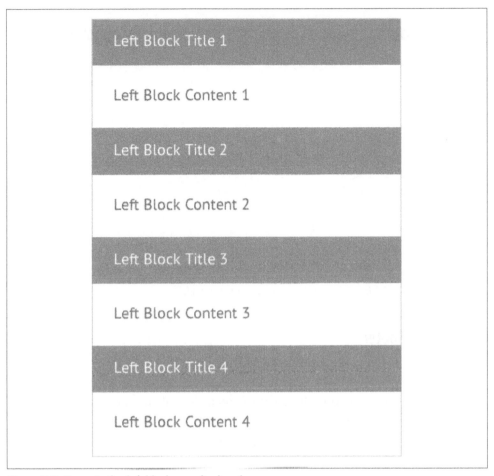

Figure 2-2. Four similar left blocks are displayed

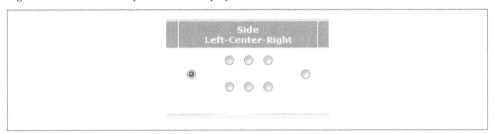

Figure 2-3. XOOPS 2.4 contains eight block positions, shown here

In XOOPS 2.5, we have same number of block types, but a much nicer system of block management. You can drag and drop, enable, or disable blocks instantly (see Figure 2-4).

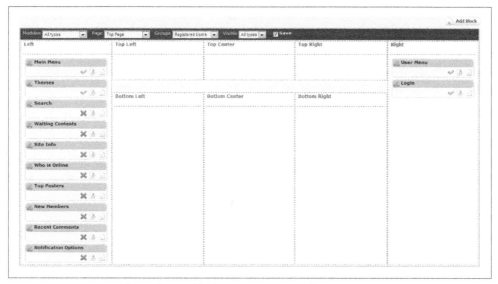

Figure 2-4. XOOPS 2.5 has a fancier block management interface

Content and Footer

If you remove all the code related to block display, there are only two lines left: <{$xoops_contents}> and <{$xoops_footer}>.

<{$xoops_contents}> is used to display the content (mainly module content). For example, the module content will be displayed when you visit a specific module.

And <{$xoops_footer}>, as the name suggests, displays a footer, such as copyright and powered-by information.

These are most of the key elements of any XOOPS theme. The major difference between XOOPS theme files and plain (X)HTML templates is basically the code above. You should already be quite familiar with HTML and CSS, and therefore designing a XOOPS theme will hopefully be intuitive for you.

In the next chapter, we will discuss how to convert an existing HTML template to XOOPS, giving you hands-on experience with XOOPS themes.

CHAPTER 3

Converting an Existing XHTML Template

OK, now you know the mechanisms of XOOPS themes. So let's get something done! In this section, you will convert an existing XHTML template into a XOOPS theme. Your focus should be the XOOPS theme syntax, not CSS.

There are lots of websites that provide free and quality CSS templates; I happened to choose *FreeCSSTemplates.org* for illustration purposes.

Get the CSS Template

Please go to *http://www.freecsstemplates.org/preview/paperslips* and get the *Paperslips* template. It is a three-column, grungy-looking template in a light color (see Figure 3-1).

Extract the archive file to *XOOPS/themes/*. After this, you should see a *paperslip* folder in *XOOPS/themes/*. If you don't like this name, you can change it. But for simplicity's sake, I will keep the original name here.

The files in the folder are shown in Figure 3-2.

Now please recall what we talked about in the last chapter regarding the XOOPS theme engine: the main theme file should be named *theme.html*. Simply change *index.html* to *theme.html*. Go to the backend of your XOOPS installation and make *paperslips* selectable, as shown in Figure 3-3.

You should see something similar to Figure 3-4.

Figure 3-1. The Paperslips template

Figure 3-2. The files in the paperslip folder

Figure 3-3. Making the Paperslips theme selectable

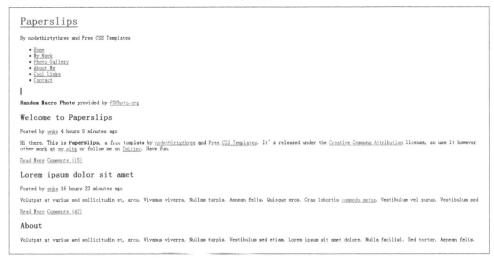

Figure 3-4. Don't panic if you see this! You're still doing it right.

"What have I done wrong?" you might ask. Actually, you've done everything right. You just need one further fix.

Perhaps you've realized what is the problem here: the paths. The paths in the original files might not fit, and an amendment is needed. Open *theme.html*, and in Line 8 where the stylesheet path is defined,

```
<link href="style.css" rel="stylesheet" type="text/css" media="all" />
```

change style.css to **<{xoImgUrl style.css}>**.

Save the file and refresh your browser, and things should look like Figure 3-5.

See? It is all right now. <{xoImgUrl style.css}> is actually equivalent to *http://yourxoops.com/themes/paperslips/style.css*. It will be interpreted as such by the XOOPS theme engine.

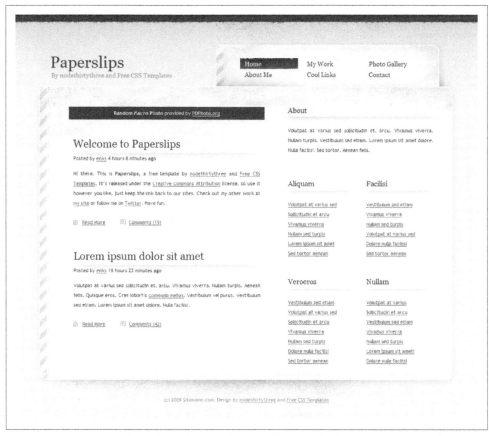

Figure 3-5. Once you've fixed the paths, your browser should look like this upon being refreshed

Plug It into XOOPS

Well, now the template is correctly displayed in your XOOPS installation. The next step is to integrate the template. We need to replace some of the content with XOOPS theme engine syntax. It might be a little abstract at first, but don't worry.

Please go to the content inside `<div id="content">`.

It is easy to discover that this code is actually the main content area of the template. What you need to do is to replace this with the XOOPS center block code.

First, let's remove the `<div class="photo">...</div>`, as we don't need it for now. Recall the structure that you learned in the last chapter:

```
<!-- CENTER -->
<{foreach item=block from=$xoBlocks.page_topcenter}>
<{$block.title}>
```

```
<{$block.content}>
<{/foreach}>
```

We'll use the *center center* (sometimes referred to as *top center*) block as an example. Looking at the Paperslips template, you can intuit that we will add some tags to our basic structure to "fit in."

```
<!-- CENTER -->
<{foreach item=block from=$xoBlocks.page_topcenter}>
    <div class="title"><h2><{$block.title}></h2></div>
    <div class="entry"><{$block.content}></div>
<{/foreach}>
```

You can do this for other center blocks. Please do not forget the `<{$xoops_contents}>`.

After you've done everything, save your *theme.html* and refresh your browser, and you will see the center blocks you've set up in XOOPS.

If you don't see the update, please go to *System Options→ Preferences→General Settings*, and set *Check templates for modifications* to *Yes* (as shown in Figure 3-6). You should have no problem then.

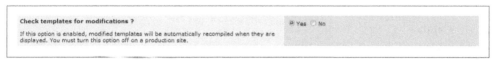

Figure 3-6. Set "Check templates for modifications" to "Yes" if your browser does not properly show the update

I will illustrate this technique again, using a sidebar as an example.

Please find the line containing `<div id="sidebar">`. (I cannot tell you the line number, as you've already modified the theme when you implemented the center blocks.)

By preliminary investigation, you can see that:

- `<div class="section1">` controls the upper part of the sidebar.
- `<div class="section2">` controls the left part.
- `<div class="section3">` controls the right part.

You might ask, "How do you know that?" I find out by researching *style.css*. However, even without knowing anything about CSS, you can figure this out by comparing the content in your browser to that in your editor. It works 99% of the time (except when the template author uses the same text for all parts).

Suppose you want to use the following block-matching relationship:

Section 1 Leave it there, we don't need that for now.
Section 2 Left block
Section 3 Right block

Recall the basic structure for the left block:

```
<{foreach item=block from=$xoBlocks.canvas_left}>
    <{$block.title}>
    <{$block.content}>
<{/foreach}>
```

You should add the following markup:

```
<{foreach item=block from=$xoBlocks.canvas_left}>
<li>
<h2><{$block.title}></h2>
    <{$block.content}>
</li>
<{/foreach}>
```

The code within `<div class="section2">` should look like this:

```
<div class="section2">
    <ul>
        <{foreach item=block from=$xoBlocks.canvas_left}>
        <li>
            <h2><{$block.title}></h2>
            <{$block.content}>
        </li>
        <{/foreach}>
    </ul>
</div>
```

Please pay attention to the placement of `<ul>` and `<li>` tags.

Similarly, we can fit in the right blocks. Up to now, XOOPS blocks should be displayed correctly in your theme.

Further Modifications

The theme is 80% complete. But there are a few more things to do.

Head Part

I strongly suggest that you replace the code within `<head>` with the code in the blank theme in the previous chapter. This will save you a lot of effort and will work 99% of the time:

```
<head>
<meta http-equiv="content-type" content="text/html; charset=<{$xoops_charset}>" />
<meta http-equiv="content-language" content="<{$xoops_langcode}>" />
<meta name="robots" content="<{$xoops_meta_robots}>" />
<meta name="keywords" content="<{$xoops_meta_keywords}>" />
<meta name="description" content="<{$xoops_meta_description}>" />
<meta name="rating" content="<{$xoops_meta_rating}>" />
<meta name="author" content="<{$xoops_meta_author}>" />
<meta name="copyright" content="<{$xoops_meta_copyright}>" />
<meta name="generator" content="XOOPS" />
```

```
<title><{$xoops_sitename}> - <{$xoops_pagetitle}></title>
<link href="<{$xoops_url}>favicon.ico" rel="SHORTCUT ICON" />
<link rel="stylesheet" type="text/css" media="screen"
    href="<{$xoops_url}>xoops.css" />
<link rel="stylesheet" type="text/css" media="screen" href="<{$xoops_themecss}>" />
<{$xoops_module_header}>
</head>
```

XOOPS will replace those Smarty variables with the correct content set in the system. This is an essential step for Search Engine Optimization (SEO).

Logo and Navigation Bar

You might find that the logo is *not* your XOOPS site name. Please find the following code:

```
<div id="logo">
    <h1><a href="#">Paperslips</a></h1>
    <p>By nodethirtythree and Free CSS Templates</p>
</div>
```

And replace it with:

```
<div id="logo">
    <h1><a href="#"><{$xoops_sitename}></a></h1>
    <p><{$xoops_slogan}></p>
</div>
```

Again, you can see that the aim is to replace the text in the template with Smarty variables that can be used by XOOPS.

You can modify the navigation bar according to the modules that you've installed. Some advanced techniques will be introduced in later chapters.

Footer

Add `<{$xoops_footer}>` to the code within `<div id="footer" class="container">`.

Please do not remove the credit to the original author. We need to comply with the license and respect the work of the designer.

Since XOOPS is released under GPL 2.0, you could remove the "Powered by XOOPS" line, but the XOOPS community would highly appreciate it if you preserve the footer.

The Last Fix to Make the Theme Work

Figure 3-7 shows the last *obvious* problem: the items in *User Menu* and *Main Menu* do not appear in a list.

Figure 3-7. The menu items run together in a paragraph instead of a list

This is because the style of the *Main Menu* and *User Menu* are not defined in *style.css*, but it is not difficult to fix this.

Please open *style.css*, and at the end of the file, add the following code:

```
#usermenu a, #mainmenu a {
    display: block;
}
```

Save your file and refresh: you should see results similar to those shown in Figure 3-8.

Figure 3-8. After fixing the display, the menu items now appear as a list

The theme will now work on your XOOPS website. That's basically all you need to do with *theme.html*. However, you might find that in certain pages, some styles seem to be missing. We will need to modify *style.css* to define those styles.

You can get the source code for the theme in its current state (though we will perfect the theme later on) from *http://insraq.me/files/book/paperslips_ch3.zip*.

CHAPTER 4

Styling XOOPS and Creating a Theme from 960

This chapter mainly deals with how to add more styles to your themes. We will continue to use the theme you converted in Chapter 3. Also, we will discuss how to create a theme from the 960 CSS Framework for XOOPS (found online at *http://code.google .com/p/insraq/source/browse/#svn%2Ftrunk%2F960*) to save you time and coding.

More on Styling XOOPS

If you find an existing XOOPS theme and open the *style.css* file for that theme, you will find lots of CSS definitions. If the file is not well commented, though, you can hardly decipher what they actually do. It is the same when you write your own CSS file: if you do not follow a certain procedure, you will confuse others (and maybe even yourself).

There are lots of ways to categorize the definitions. I will introduce a method that I use when I am writing XOOPS themes.

Global Style

These definitions regard general tags, like body, a, img, h1-h6, etc. They will be used extensively on every page. Only include those styles that are applicable to every page (for example, if you want a link on a specific page to be red, do *not* write color: red; here).

Theme-Specific Style

These definitions are usually CSS definitions used by *theme.html* (for example, header, content, footer, slideshow, block, and so on). These styles are not used by XOOPS by default; they are used by your theme.

I originally used some general naming conventions like "nav" and "menu". Then I found out that this may cause conflict between theme style (your *style.css*) and module style (some module-specific styles defined by module developers).

It is best to add a prefix to these names, like "inspire10-nav" and "inspire10-menu". This way, even though we have longer names, there will be fewer conflicts and more distinction.

XOOPS System Template Style

These definitions are used by the XOOPS system template and are supposed to be used by modules—for example, the System menus and User menus. Others include very detailed table style definitions and form definitions. (Strictly speaking, forms are not really in this category, but for convenience, we will include them here.)

Dealing with XOOPS Template Style

Global style and *theme-specific style* are not XOOPS-specific, meaning that you should write them by the time you finish your XHTML and CSS templates. To include them in your theme, simply copy and paste.

The XOOPS system template style (referred to as *required style* therein) is generally not defined in your original template, but is required by XOOPS. This is what you need to work on.

XOOPS has many historical versions. Each version might have different requirements for required styles. I will introduce the common ones and leave those that are rarely used for you to discover on your own later.

#MainMenu

This group of style definitions is used by the system module on the *main menu* (usually used as the *navigation menu*). They are all under #mainmenu ID, and have different classes:

```
style.css (excerpt)
#mainmenu {}
#mainmenu a {
    display: block;
}
#mainmenu a:hover {}
#mainmenu a:active, #mainmenu a.current {}
#mainmenu a:visited {}
#mainmenu a.menuTop  {}
#mainmenu a.menuMain {}
#mainmenu a.menuSub {
    padding: 0 0 0 10px;
```

```
}
#mainmenu a.menuSub:hover  {}
#mainmenu a.maincurrent {}
```

Above is the necessary definition. As you can see, I only added two definitions (a and a.menuSub) and left the others blank. The display: block; is used to make the menu item displayed in the block, and the definition in #mainmenu a.menuSub is used to differentiate subitems from main items. I added a 10px left padding to achieve this.

#Usermenu

usermenu is quite similar to mainmenu, except that there is no "subitem" in usermenu:

```
style.css (excerpt)
#usermenu {}
#usermenu a {
    display: block;
}
#usermenu a:hover  {}
#usermenu a:active, #usermenu a.current {}
#usermenu a:visited {}
#usermenu a.menuTop {}
#usermenu a.highlight {}
```

Table and Cells

This is the most complex part. XOOPS has a complicated definition of *table style*, and different modules might use themes differently. I always try to maintain a minimum definition that works well in most situations, and let the modules set their styles. But the problem remains unsolved:

```
style.css (excerpt)
table {
    width:100%;
    margin: .5em 0 1em 0;
    border-collapse: collapse;
}

th {
    font-weight: bold;
    text-align: center;
    vertical-align : middle;
    background: #e7eef7;
    padding: 5px;
}

tr {
    border: 1px solid #eee;
}

td {
    padding: 5px;
}
```

```css
.outer {
    border-collapse: collapse;
    padding: 5px;
}

.head {
    font-weight: bold;
    vertical-align: top;
    background: #f8f8f8;
}

.even {
    padding: 5px;
    border: 1px solid #eee;
}

.odd {
    padding: 5px;
    border: 1px solid #eee;
    background: #e7eef7;
}
```

The above code is the style I use in the 960 CSS framework for XOOPS. I make a lot of assumptions about styles here. The border of the table is #eeeeee, and for th (which defines a style for table headers) and .head (which defines a style for the head class), I add a background to differentiate them. I also add a padding of 5px to td (which defines a style for standard table cells) and additional classes.

I do it this way because I think table definitions should not be the focus of theme design, and shouldn't bother designers so much. When I first designed for XOOPS, I was quite confused by those table definitions. They seemed too overwhelmed with details. Even if you do not define style for most of the selectors, you will be fine.

Another problem is that different module designers will use different markup for their modules. For example, some will use <th> as a table header, while others use <th class="header">. So my current approach is to define a set of minimum styles. But a better way to tackle this would be for the XOOPS community to work out a standard for module templates. If all the designers and developers followed this standard, differing markup would no longer be a problem.

Smarty: I Want to Know More

XOOPS provides a lot of Smarty variables to help designers achieve their goals. Here, I've made a list of the commonly used Smarty variables according to my experience over the past few years. I've categorized them for easy reference.

Header Tags

`<{$xoops_charset}>`

Output the character set information (e.g., "iso-8859-1", "UTF-8").

`<{$xoops_langcode}>`

Output content language (e.g., "DE", "EN").

`<{$xoops_meta_keywords}>`

Output the keyword list from the Meta/Footer settings.

`<{$xoops_meta_description}>`

Output the meta tag site description.

`<{$meta_copyright}>`

Output the meta tag copyright text.

`<{$meta_robots}>`

Output the W3C robot meta tag info.

`<{$meta_rating}>`

Output the meta tag rating information.

`<{$xoops_js}>`

Output XOOPS JavaScript.

`<{$xoops_module_header}>`

Output the module header. Usually, the module's own JavaScript will be output-ted. Details will be explained later.

XOOPS General

`<{$xoops_sitename}>`

Output the site name.

`<{$xoops_slogan}>`

Output the site slogan.

`<{$xoops_pagetitle}>`

Output the page title.

`<{$xoops_theme}>`

Output theme's name in directory "/themes/" (e.g., "default", "suico").

`<{$xoops_dirname}>`

Output the name of the current module directory. If no module is displayed, this value is set to "system".

`<{$xoops_themecss}>`

Inserts the *style.css* file (e.g., "*http://www.xoops.org/themes/default/style.css*").

`<{xoImgUrl}>`

This is the XOOPS resource locator. It is often used if you want to link to an image or a CSS. Detailed usage will be explained throughout the book.

`<{$xoops_url}>` or `<{xoAppUrl}>`
Output the site URL (e.g., "*http://www.xoops.org*"), without the final slash.

`<{$xoops_banner}>`
Display banners.

`<{$xoops_contents}>`
Display the news and other content.

`<{$xoops_footer}>`
Display the footer.

`<{$xoops_requesturi}>`
Request URL provided by XOOPS (e.g., */modules/news/article.php?storyid=1*).

XOOPS User-Related

`<{$xoops_isadmin}>`
Test if the visitor is Administrator—return TRUE if yes.

`<{$xoops_isuser}>`
Test if the visitor is a logged in user—return TRUE if yes.

`<{$xoops_userid}>`
User ID of the member.

`<{$xoops_uname}>`
Username for the member.

Smarty Flow Control

`<{if $smarty_variable}>`
...
`<{elseif}>`
...
`<{else}>`
...
`<{/if}>`
The `if-else` control.

`<{foreach item=block from=$xoBlocks.canvas_left}>`
`<{/foreach}>`
The `foreach` loop.

There is also a `foreachq`, described next.

`<{foreachq item=block from=$xoBlocks.canvas_left}>`
...
`<{/foreach}>`
Note that the closing tag is `<{/foreach}>` instead of `<{/foreachq}>`.

Include and Assign

`<{include file=PATH}>` or `<{includeq file=PATH}>`
>   Used to include a file in *theme.html*; the difference is that the latter is more efficient (but less secure).

`<{assign var=NAME value=SOME_VALUE}>`
>   Assign a value to a Smarty variable. For example:

```
<{assign var=theme_name value=$xoTheme->folderName}>
<{assign var=theme_name value=$xoTheme->folderName|cat:'/tpl'}>
```

Then you could use:

```
<{includeq file="$theme_name/tpl.html"}>
```

This would include *XOOPS/themes/yourtheme_tpl.html* or *XOOPS/themes/tpl/yourtheme_tpl.html*.

More on Smarty: Tricks and Examples

Module-Based Navigation

Now suppose you have a typical site navigation markup:

```
<ul class="nav">
    <li class="current"><a href="#">Home</a></li>
    <li><a href="#">News</a></li>
    <li><a href="#">Forum</a></li>
    <li><a href="#">Blogs</a></li>
    <li><a href="#">Contact</a></li>
</ul>
```

You want the navigation panel to tell the visitor which section of the website they are currently in. The most common way is to add a current class to the current item. Then you can style the class in your CSS file.

The trick is to add a current class to the current item. How does one achieve that in XOOPS? It's easy:

```
<ul class="nav">
    <li<{if $xoops_dirname == "system"}> class="current"<{/if}>>
        <a href="#">Home</a>
    </li>
    <li<{if $xoops_dirname == "news"}> class="current"<{/if}>>
        <a href="#">News</a>
    </li>
    <li<{if $xoops_dirname == "forum"}> class="current"<{/if}>>
        <a href="#">Forum</a>
    </li>
    <li<{if $xoops_dirname == "xpress"}> class="current"<{/if}>>
        <a href="#">Blogs</a>
    </li>
```

```
        <li<{if $xoops_dirname == "contact"}> class="current"<{/if}>>
            <a href="#">Contact</a>
        </li>
    </ul>
```

As mentioned earlier, `$xoops_dirname` outputs the current module directory name. Suppose you are using News module; the corresponding directory name is *news*. So we can use an `if` clause in Smarty to test whether `$xoops_dirname` equals the current module name. If yes, then we add a `current` class.

What About a Block Without a Title?

Usually, a block consists of a block title and block content. However, for some blocks, you may think the block title is meaningless and you probably do not want to display it. Take a look at our previous markup. If the block does not have a block title, the output will look like this:

```
<div class="title"><h2></h2></div>
<div class="entry">This is the block content</div>
```

This does not look nice. If you define some style for the title, it will simply give a blank result.

A better way to handle this is to only show the markup for the block title when the block has a title:

```
<{if $block.title}>
    <div class="title"><h2></h2></div>
<{/if}>
<div class="entry">This is the block content</div>
```

Use the above markup, and if a block has no title (i.e., the block title is empty), the output will look like this:

```
<div class="entry">This is the block content</div>
```

The markup for a block title will not be output.

Custom Block Filter

This sounds like rocket science, but it really isn't. This trick follows the previous workaround. Suppose you want to have a special markup or style for some specific blocks —for example, the *Search* block. You have two choices. The first is the *block anywhere* technique, which will be covered in Chapter 7. This is fairly complex and is suitable for a situation in which your whole website is made of custom-designed blocks.

The second choice is to create a *custom block filter*. This is easy, and applies to situations in which you only have one or two custom-designed blocks.

To illustrate, look at the original code for blocks:

```
<{foreach item=block from=$xoBlocks.page_topcenter}>
<div class="title"><h2><{$block.title}></h2></div>
<div class="entry"><{$block.content}></div>
<{/foreach}>
```

A block filter is simply an `if` clause:

```
<{foreach item=block from=$xoBlocks.page_topcenter}>
    <{if $block.title == "Search"}>
        <div class="block-search">
    <{else}>
        <div class="block-general">
    <{/if}>
        <div class="title"><h2><{$block.title}></h2></div>
        <div class="entry"><{$block.content}></div>
    </div>
<{/foreach}>
```

With the above code, if the block title is `"Search"`, then we will apply a `block-search` class to the block, and then apply the `block-general` class.

To add more than one filter, use an `if-elseif` clause:

```
<{foreach item=block from=$xoBlocks.page_topcenter}>
    <{if $block.title == "Search"}>
        <div class="block-search">
    <{elseif $block.title == "Welcome"}>
        <div class="block-welcome">
    <{elseif}>
        <div class="block-general">
    <{/if}>
        <div class="title"><h2><{$block.title}></h2></div>
        <div class="entry"><{$block.content}></div>
    </div>
<{/foreach}>
```

Blocks can be filtered not only by names, but also by `id`s, a technique which is less commonly used:

```
<{foreach item=block from=$xoBlocks.page_topcenter}>
    <{if $block.id == 5}>
        <div class="block-search">
    <{elseif $block.id == 6}>
        <div class="block-welcome">
    <{elseif}>
        <div class="block-general">
    <{/if}>
        <div class="title"><h2><{$block.title}></h2></div>
        <div class="entry"><{$block.content}></div>
    </div>
<{/foreach}>
```

"What is my block ID?" you may ask.

The *ID* of a block can be found out in the following way: edit a block, and in the address bar of your browser, you will see a URL like this:

```
http://example.com/modules/system/admin.php?fct=blocksadmin&op=edit&bid=1
```

The *bid* part of the query string is your block ID.

Create a Theme with 960

To create a theme from scratch takes a lot of time, which is why the concept of a framework is so handy. There are two types of framework, and both have their pros and cons. One is very rigid and strict, with lots of rules and conventions. The learning curve is very steep, but once you master it, you can write very concise and beautiful code.

Another type is loosely organized. It provides lots of functions to help your design. But even if you don't follow all of the conventions, it's fine. The learning curve is flat, but you'll probably need to write more code than with the first type.

When I first decided to create a theme framework for XOOPS, there were already many other good frameworks. (One of the most famous is Morphogenesis, created by Chris (*kris_fr* in the forums). It is very powerful, concentrating on the file structure and functions. It does have some documentation, but is a little difficult for beginners.)

I decided to create a theme framework that focuses on design itself. I did not provide a lot of functions within it. The framework includes a *theme.html* to set home page structure using the 960 CSS Framework; some CSS files with definitions necessary to create a theme; and some other must-have JavaScript libraries.

To create a theme with 960, just copy the folder, rename it, and it's done!

Then, open *theme.html* and you can see that the home page structure is written in 960, which assumes a width of 960 pixels and provides a grid system based on frequently used dimensions. If you are familiar with this system, you can easily modify it. If not, just leave it there, because the default grid layout will work 90% of the time.

The next step is to add some selectors in *theme.html* and add the corresponding styles to *style.css*. Your style definitions should be added in the `/* Theme Specific Style */` section. Assuming you are already used to designing in CSS, you will have no trouble dealing with rest of the stuff in the template—it's just like designing pure XHTML and CSS templates, except for some Smarty syntax. If the syntax throws you at all, refer back to Chapter 2.

jQuery and UI Libraries for XOOPS Themes

Several years ago, when I needed to add animations to my web design, Flash was the first word that came into my mind. But nowadays, with the rapid development of Java-Script and its related libraries, I seldom use Flash in general web design. JavaScript has taken over many roles that used to be filled by Flash. In this chapter, I will cover how to use one of the most popular JavaScript libraries, jQuery, in XOOPS themes.

Link Your Theme to jQuery

The first method that comes to your mind should be adding:

```
<script src=" https://ajax.googleapis.com/ajax/libs/jQuery/1.6/jQuery.min.js"
    type="text/javascript"></script>
```

to the <head> section of *theme.html*.

This is very intuitive, and will work without too many disturbances. But you may ask: What disturbances might we encounter?

Look back at "A Simple Example" on page 6 in Chapter 2, where I first introduced a bare bones theme. You might notice that there is a <{$xoops_module_header}> in the <head> section. This tells XOOPS to load the header required by specific modules—which allows a module to load what it needs on demand, instead of loading the files for the whole of XOOPS.

A common example is an editor's JavaScript and stylesheet. As jQuery is very popular, many modules will load jQuery on demand. However, if you use the above code to load jQuery in your theme, it will be loaded *again* for some modules, thus causing some malfunctions (such errors will only happen in modules that load jQuery on demand, but not for the whole of XOOPS).

Trabis has provided a technique at *http://bit.ly/91pH6t* (please note that there is a small typo in the original code) to tackle this obstacle. Instead of directly adding <{$xoops_module_header}>, we add:

```
<{php}>
    global $xoTheme;
$xoTheme->addScript('browse.php?Frameworks/jQuery/jQuery.js');
$this->assign('xoops_module_header',
$xoTheme->renderMetas(null, true));
<{/php}>
<{$xoops_module_header}>
```

The above code does the following:

- Loads jQuery to your theme if it has not already been loaded by a module.
- Avoids loading jQuery twice to your theme if it *has* already been loaded by a module.

Note that after version 2.4, XOOPS provides jQuery support by default, so we can simply load jQuery from XOOPS:

```
$xoTheme->addScript('browse.php?Frameworks/jQuery/jQuery.js');
```

Now you can use jQuery in your theme.

Using jQuery in a XOOPS template is basically the same as using it in static HTML pages. However, since XOOPS template uses the Smarty engine, we can integrate jQuery into the template engine to achieve more complex effects.

In the following sections, I will use two cases to illustrate how to make use of jQuery. The first case involves using it separately—not integrated with the template engine. The second case takes advantage of integration.

Case1: jQuery Used Separately (Adding a Slider to Your Theme)

A *slider*, or a sliding block, usually works as shown in Figure 5-1 (the screenshots from Figure 5-1 and Figure 5-2 come from one of my themes, InsApp).

Figure 5-1. A sliding block is hidden until the user clicks the arrow in the upper right-hand corner

When you click the upper-right arrow, a hidden block will slide down and appear, as shown in Figure 5-2.

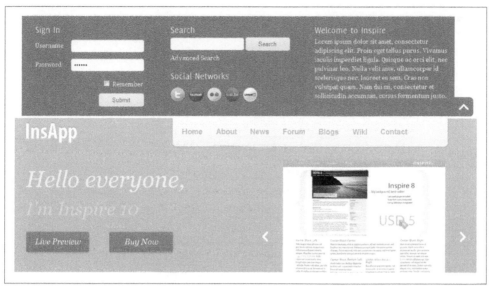

Figure 5-2. The block that had previously been hidden is now revealed, and the arrow may be used to hide it again

Now the arrow on the right that had been pointing down becomes an up arrow, and you can click it to slide the block back up.

This sort of sliding block is a fairly common effect used by many modern websites for login or other information that doesn't need to be presented to first-time visitors, yet should be easily accessible.

If you are very familiar with jQuery in other settings, you can easily implement this in your XOOPS theme: it is basically the same. But I will demonstrate this step by step. Let's use the "Paperslips" template that we converted in Chapter 3.

Get the Graphics Done

You might need some graphics, like arrows, icons, and a background.

In Paperslips, you can see a textured, dark red header (labeled 1 in Figure 5-3), where you may add a light, textured background slider. Another possible choice would be to extend the dark red header. I will carry out the former option for illustration purposes.

First, you will need to redo the textures. To accomplish this, we can make use of *bg05.jpg* in the *images* folder.

Figure 5-3. At the top of the window, a dark red header labeled by the numeral 1 shows where we will add a sliding block

Then you might want to make two arrows in your favorite graphic editor. However, for simplicity, I will use some text in the navigation panel instead of arrows.

Now that we're ready with the graphics, let's code the (X)HTML and CSS.

Coding (X)HTML and CSS

We will add something before `wrapper` `div`. Let's call it `slider`:

```
theme.html (excerpt)
<div id="slider">
    <div class="slidercontent">
        <h2>Lorem ipsum dolor sit amet</h2>
        Lorem ipsum dolor sit amet, consectetur adipiscing elit. Vivamus turpis
        lacus, sagittis a cursus a, ornare dictum mauris. Etiam ultricies turpis
        eget tortor congue interdum. Morbi lacinia libero at felis vestibulum
        malesuada. Vestibulum ante ipsum primis in faucibus orci luctus et ultrices
        posuere cubilia Curae; Maecenas eget imperdiet augue. Nunc nec malesuada
        neque. Phasellus sed est turpis, et tincidunt dolor.
    </div>
</div>
```

Now add a CSS definition to *style.css*:

```
style.css (excerpt)
/* Slider */
#slider {
    width: 965px;
    margin: 0 auto;
    background: url(images/bg05.jpg) repeat-x;
    background-position: bottom;
}

.slidercontent {
    padding: 20px 30px 20px 80px;
}
```

Refresh your browser...not bad. You might have even better ideas, so please go ahead and try them out. For illustration, I will go with this version, shown in Figure 5-4.

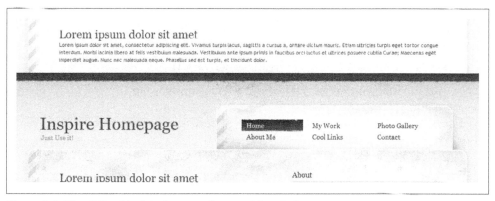

Figure 5-4. The sliding block is shown at the top of the window

Next, we should add the toggle switch.

I decided to use the third item in the navigation panel as the switch (I am so lazy!). So I change:

```
<li><a href="#">Photo Gallery</a></li>
```

to:

```
<li><a href="#">Toggle Header</a></li>
```

The XHTML and CSS coding is done. It seems simple, because I just want to achieve a simple effect. Of course, you can play around with other implementations that yield much fancier effects. The point here is to illustrate that implementing a jQuery effect in a XOOPS theme is basically the same as in other static HTML templates.

Read through the code again, and you will notice that if you copied it to a static HTML file, it would work there, too. It should also work if you simply copy the code from HTML to XOOPS.

Adding jQuery Effect

If you are with me so far, the next section will be relatively easy.

Add `display: none;` to your `#slider` in *style.css*; now it should look like this:

```
#slider {
    width: 965px;
    margin: 0 auto;
    background: url(images/bg05.jpg) repeat-x;
    background-position: bottom;
    display: none;
}
```

Then, add `id="slidertoggle"` to your toggle switch:

```
<li><a id="slidertoggle" href="#">Toggle Header</a></li>
```

Lastly, add the following script right before the closing `body` tag:

```
<script type="text/javascript">
$('#slidertoggle').click(function () {
    $('#slider').slideToggle('slow');
});
</script>
```

Ta-da...all done! It isn't too hard, is it?

Now refresh your browser to see the result. When you first load the page, the sliding block will not be shown (see Figure 5-5).

Then click the text that says "Toggle Header" in the upper-right corner, and the sliding block will slide down, as shown in Figure 5-6.

Click on the text again, and the block will slide up.

Once again, I must say that the effect I implemented here is—to some extent—crude. But the point is to show you that you can easily transfer your knowledge of designing static HTML to designing a XOOPS theme. Some designers are intimidated by XOOPS and its template engine. After this example, I hope you will feel more confident about designing for XOOPS.

Figure 5-5. Our home page looks mostly the same as it did before

Figure 5-6. When the user clicks the "Toggle Header" text in the navigation panel, our sliding block appears

Case2: jQuery Integration (Transform Your Blocks into Tabs)

The jQuery library is very powerful. If we integrate jQuery into XOOPS, we can achieve much more sophisticated effects. The integration you are able to carry out will be based on your understanding of the XOOPS template engine. I will not simply tell you how to implement this. Instead, I will try to present the idea behind it: how to come up with the integration. You will be able to derive many other methods based on a little bit of theory.

In this case study, I will implement a Tab in a XOOPS theme, which can be controlled by block management of XOOPS.

jQuery Tools as UI Library

Of course, you can write your own tab implementation in jQuery, but who has the time? There are many excellent JavaScript programmers who have already done this. Why not make use of their work instead of reinventing the wheel?

You could use jQuery UI, which is the official UI library for jQuery—but jQuery UI is too big, and I only need a tab implementation. So in this example, I will pick jQuery Tools (*http://flowplayer.org/tools/index.html*). It is much smaller, and has very good documentation and demonstrations available. We will continue to use the Paperslips theme.

Create a folder called *js* in your *theme* folder. Download the `jQuery Tools Tabs` module. By default, the file name is *tabs.min.js*. Put it in the *js* folder (see Figure 5-7).

Figure 5-7. The jQuery Tabs module will transform blocks into tabs

Then open *theme.html*, and add a link to *tabs.min.js* using the approach I introduced at the beginning of this chapter:

```php
<{php}>
    global $xoTheme;
    $xoTheme->addScript('browse.php?Frameworks/jQuery/jQuery.js');
    $xoTheme->addScript('js/tabs.min.js');
    $header = empty($GLOBALS['xoopsOption']['xoops_module_header']) ?
    $this->get_template_vars('xoops_module_header') :
    $GLOBALS['xoopsOption']['xoops_module_header'];
    $this->assign('xoops_module_header', $xoTheme->renderMetas(null, true) . $header);
<{/php}>
<{$xoops_module_header}>
```

The line in bold is what you need to add.

Implementing Tabs Separately

Now what you should do is to implement tabs separately, just as we discussed in our Case 1 study earlier in this chapter. If you need to, you can refer to the documentation here: *http://flowplayer.org/tools/demos/tabs/index.html*

In this example, I will use the third implementation on this page: *http://flowplayer.org/tools/demos/tabs/skins.html*, that is, "Tab skin without images". Again, my purpose here is not to make some fancy tabs, but to present the integration method and the idea behind it. So I've chosen one with minimal styles.

By looking at the source code of the demo page, you can find out that Tabs have a basic HTML structure. Copy and paste the following to your XOOPS theme after `<div id="content">`:

```
theme.html (excerpt)
<!-- tabs -->
<ul class="css-tabs">
    <li><a href="#">Tab 1</a></li>
    <li><a href="#">Tab 2</a></li>
    <li><a href="#">Tab 3</a></li>
</ul>

<!-- panes -->
<div class="css-panes">
    <div>
        Tab 1 Content
    </div>

    <div>
        Tab 2 Content
    </div>

    <div>
        Tab 3 Content
    </div>
</div>
```

You will also need to add the following before the closing of the body tag:

```
$(".css-tabs").tabs(".css-panes > div");
```

If you followed what we did in Case 1, then right before the `</body>` tag you should have some code like this:

```
<script type="text/javascript">
// Tabs
$(".css-tabs").tabs(".css-panes > div");
// Header Slider
$('#slidertoggle').click(function () {
    $('#slider').slideToggle('slow');
});
</script>
```

And that's not the end. We still need to add styles. The CSS file provided by the jQuery Tools document can be found here: *http://flowplayer.org/tools/css/tabs-no-images.css*.

Save it as *tabs.css* and use the `@import` rule to include it in *style.css*.

Save all the files and refresh your browser, and you should see that the tab is actually working (though not necessarily looking good—see Figure 5-8).

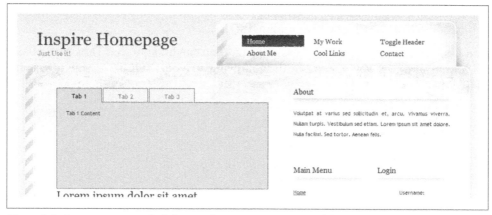

Figure 5-8. As you can see on the left, our tabs are now appearing, although they are not yet very stylish

I've gone through this very quickly, as it is pretty much just a replication of what we did in the Case 1 study.

Integration: How to Come Up with an Idea

Look at the HTML code of *Tabs* again. What does it remind you of?

```
<!-- tabs -->
<ul class="css-tabs">
    <li><a href="#">Tab 1</a></li>
    <li><a href="#">Tab 2</a></li>
    <li><a href="#">Tab 3</a></li>
</ul>

<!-- panes -->
<div class="css-panes">
    <div>
        Tab 1 Content
    </div>

    <div>
        Tab 2 Content
    </div>
```

```
    <div>
        Tab 3 Content
    </div>
</div>
```

Did you notice that the structure is similar to some of the structures we have already come across? I will give you a hint: read the XOOPS block structure code again (from the section "Block-Displaying Structures" on page 8).

We can actually rewrite the *Tab* structure like this:

```
<!-- tabs -->
<ul class="css-tabs">
    <li><a href="#">Block 1 Title</a></li>
    <li><a href="#">Block 2 Title</a></li>
    <li><a href="#">Block 3 Title</a></li>
</ul>

<!-- panes -->
<div class="css-panes">
    <div>
        Block 1 Content
    </div>

    <div>
        Block 2 Content
    </div>

    <div>
        Block 3 Content
    </div>
</div>
```

The difference is that block content does not directly follow block titles. They are separated and then grouped together.

I suggest you stop reading for a moment and think of a way to integrate tabs into the block system. I've given you lots of hints already.

Integration: How to Implement the Idea

Here is my implementation. You might have your own ideas, so go ahead with those and come back later to compare with mine. You might come up with a better way.

Suppose I want to integrate tabs with center blocks (or *top center*, to be consistent with XOOPS naming). This is the original code for the center block:

```
<!-- CENTER -->
<{foreach item=block from=$xoBlocks.page_topcenter}>
    <div class="title"><h2><{$block.title}></h2></div>
    <div class="entry"><{$block.content}></div>
<{/foreach}>
```

As we know, `<{foreach item=block from=$xoBlocks.page_topcenter}>` is used as a loop. So what we need to do is to loop both the block title and the block content and fit them into the *Tabs* structure. It looks like this (please pay attention to the code in bold):

```
<!-- CENTER -->
<!-- tabs -->
<ul class="css-tabs">
    <{foreach item=block from=$xoBlocks.page_topcenter}>
        <li><a href="#"><{$block.title}></a></li>
    <{/foreach}>
</ul>
<!-- panes -->
<div class="css-panes">
    <{foreach item=block from=$xoBlocks.page_topcenter}>
        <div><{$block.content}></div>
    <{/foreach}>
</div>
```

Save the files. Add some content to the top center block via XOOPS block management (see Figure 5-9), and give them short block titles, as the block title will be the tab title.

Figure 5-9. Use XOOPS block management to add content to the top center block

Refresh your browser and the tabs should be working now, as shown in Figure 5-10.

Although that still does not look very good, once you've finished the integration, other styling can easily be achieved by modifying CSS files.

My goal here was to show you how easy is to make such integrations. I hope you have captured the essence of integration. If so, then you should have no problem applying other jQuery effects to XOOPS.

Figure 5-10. Our tabs are now populated with content and titles

CHAPTER 6

Module Template Override

You may wonder how a basic XOOPS theme can be so small in size. It's because XOOPS themes only set the overall styles and block layout. But XOOPS-powered websites are more than that, because they are equipped with many modules. Modules are a special feature of XOOPS, which makes it highly extendable. Modules work like plug-ins to some extent, but they are far more powerful. Actually, the XOOPS core system can be viewed as a basic module.

Then there is a problem: how do you deal with the themes for different modules? XOOPS themes only set the basic styling and block layout, and allow specific modules to have their own templates—even styling—provided that the stylesheets will not clash.

Since we are now on the topic, I should pause to explain the difference between a *theme* and a *template*.

A theme in XOOPS sets the style of an entire XOOPS website. The stylesheet will be applied to the whole website, including all the modules. The theme also sets block layout.

A template in XOOPS sets the layout of a specific *part* of XOOPS. The specific part can be block content, a module page, or a forward page.

Here are some further insights into themes and templates in XOOPS:

- A theme sets the layout of *blocks*; a template sets the layout *in each of the blocks*.
- A theme sets the *style* of a module page; a template sets the *layout* of the module page.
- A theme can be seen as *a template of XOOPS blocks*.
- A theme resides in */XOOPS/theme*, while a template resides in *modules/ MODULE_NAME/templates/*

But what if you want to modify the template of a specific module in your theme? Do you have to modify the module template directly?

Well, you could achieve your goal using that approach, but it has an obvious flaw. If you want to have different templates for different themes, you would need to manually replace the template every time you switch to a new theme.

That's why XOOPS introduced a *template override*. It allows you to directly override the template of any module in your theme. You don't need to modify the module template file—you just create your new template, save it to a specific folder in your theme, and XOOPS will automatically override the original module template with the new one you've created.

An Experiment in Module Template Override

Let's begin with a simple experiment.

We'll use Contact 1.7 (*http://code.google.com/p/xuups/downloads/list*) by Trabis for our example. Download and install the module, then visit the module web page. You should see something like what's shown in Figure 6-1 (assuming you're using the Paperslips theme from previous chapters).

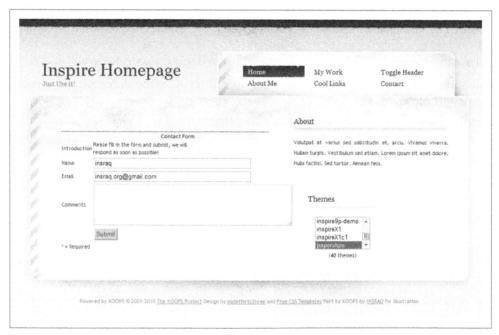

Figure 6-1. Trabis's contact module shown with the Paperslips theme

Now, let's say you want to enlarge the text "Contact Form." Please create the folder *XOOPS/themes/paperslips/modules/contact/*.

Next, copy *XOOPS/modules/contact/templates/contact_contactusform.html* to *XOOPS/themes/paperslips/modules/contact/* so that there is one HTML file in the folder you have just created.

Then edit *contact_contactusform.html*, and find the following line:

```
<th colspan="2"><{$contactform.title}></th>
```

Add an h2 tag to make it look like this:

```
<th colspan="2"><h2><{$contactform.title}></h2></th>
```

Save and refresh the browser, and it should look like Figure 6-2.

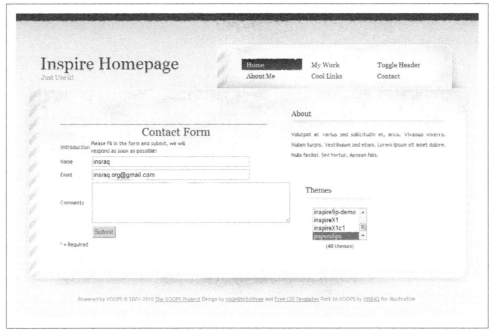

Figure 6-2. We have added an h2 tag to override the module template and enlarge some text

Let me now explain the mechanism. When a module page is loaded, XOOPS will ask for a template. Usually that would be located in *XOOPS/modules/MODULE_NAME/template*. However, XOOPS will also check *XOOPS/themes/CURRENT_THEME/modules/MODULE_NAME/* to see if there is a required template file in that folder. If the answer is yes, then XOOPS will use that instead of the one from the module itself. That's how the module template override is achieved. It's not rocket science, just a clever design.

Dig Deeper

Now, please open *contact_contactusform.html* again and read through it. What do you find? Don't you think the syntax of HTML looks very familiar? If so, you're right—it is also Smarty. This line:

```
<{foreach item=element from=$contactform.elements}>
```

is the start of a for loop. It will display every form element, just like in your theme. The difference is that in your theme, you ask XOOPS to display every block. Here, you ask XOOPS to display contact form elements.

You might notice that the code here is quite old-fashioned—it still uses a `table` layout. Let's rewrite it using XHTML and CSS.

First remove all the table elements, so it looks like this:

```
contact_contactusform.html
<{$contactform.javascript}>
<form name="<{$contactform.name}>" action="<{$contactform.action}>"
        method="<{$contactform.method}>" <{$contactform.extra}>>
    <h2><{$contactform.title}></h2>
    <!-- start of form elements loop -->
    <{foreach item=element from=$contactform.elements}>
      <{if $element.hidden != true}>
        <{$element.caption}>
        <{$element.body}>
      <{else}>
        <{$element.body}>
      <{/if}>
    <{/foreach}>
    <!-- end of form elements loop -->
</form>
```

Then, add XHTML markup and CSS definitions. You may have your own approach to accomplishing this. Here is how I did it:

```
contact_contactusform.html
<{$contactform.javascript}>
<style>
.contactform {
    margin: 0;
    padding: 0;
}
.contactform li {
    list-style: none;
    margin: 10px 0;
}
.contactform label {
    display: block;
}
</style>
<form  name="<{$contactform.name}>" action="<{$contactform.action}>"
        method="<{$contactform.method}>" <{$contactform.extra}>>
    <h2><{$contactform.title}></h2>
```

```
<!-- start of form elements loop -->
<ul class="contactform">
<{foreach item=element from=$contactform.elements}>
  <li>
      <{if $element.hidden != true}>
        <label><h3><{$element.caption}></h3></label>
        <{$element.body}>
      <{else}>
        <{$element.body}>
      <{/if}>
  </li>
<{/foreach}>
</ul>
<!-- end of form elements loop -->
</form>
```

I've bolded the part inside the foreach loop. Please note that this section of code will be repeated many times to display every form element set by the module. So the li element should be inside the foreach loop, while the ul element should stay outside. Refresh your browser to see what the contact form looks like now (or see Figure 6-3).

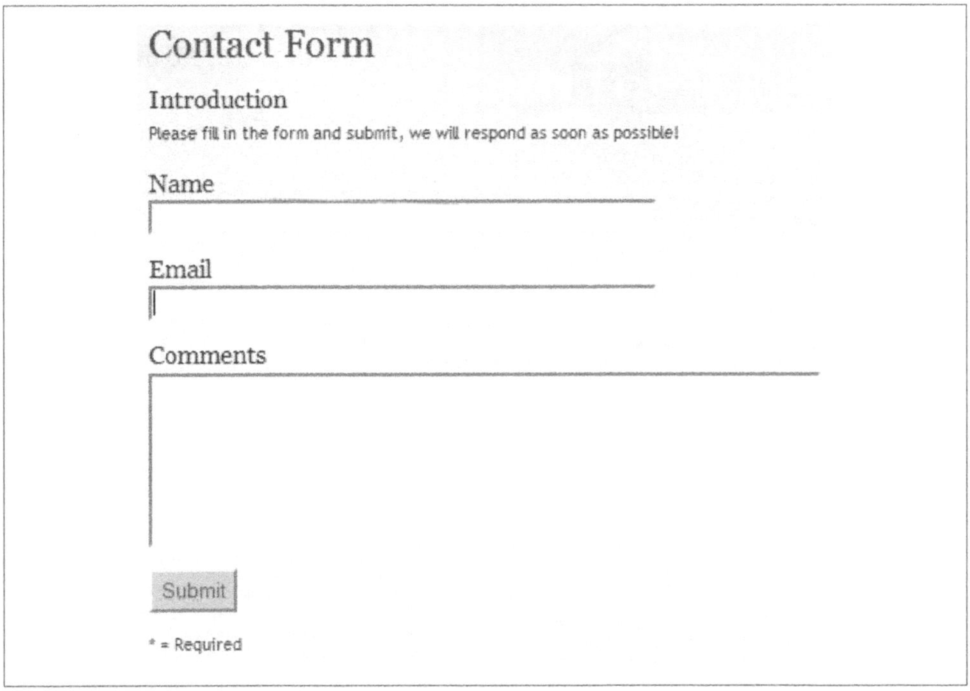

Figure 6-3. We've rewritten the contact form with XHTML and CSS instead of a table layout

Case Study: Gallery Slideshow Block

In this section, you will construct a block with a gallery slideshow. You will learn to use module override together with jQuery. It might be a bit challenging, but if you follow the steps here, you should be fine. And I hope to get you out of your comfort zone: we have been using the Paperslips theme for some time, so now let's switch to a new theme, shown in Figure 6-4: InsMinimal (*http://code.google.com/p/insraq/down loads/detail?name=InsMinimal.zip&can=2&q=*).

Figure 6-4. A page with a hard-coded slideshow shown in the InsMinimal theme

Here, we have a large slideshow, but it is hardcoded. We'll need to integrate it with a gallery module so that we can manage the slides using that gallery module.

Preparation

There are many gallery modules. I chose a widely used one called extGallery. Please get the latest version from SourceForge, at *http://sourceforge.net/projects/zoullou/files/*. I used version 1.08 for this case study.

Unzip the module and install it as usual. Since InsMinimal already has a slideshow, you just need to integrate extGallery into it. Please copy:

XOOPS/modules/extgallery/templates/blocks/extgallery_block_random.html

to:

XOOPS/themes/InsMinimal/modules/extgallery/blocks/extgallery_block_random.html

(You'll have to create the folder if it doesn't already exist.)

You may have noticed that we are overriding the module block template this time. You already know that many modules come with blocks. You can display the related blocks on the XOOPS home page by using block management. Those blocks also need a template, and by default, it is located in *XOOPS/modules/MODULE_NAME/templates/blocks*. We can also override those templates in our theme by using the same techniques.

Clean Up the Markup

Open *extgallery_block_random.html*. This is the template for "Random Photos," and you may notice that there are two foreach loops. That's because the module provides two settings of "Display Direction." We will clean up the template, preserving only the most important settings:

```
<{foreach item=photo from=$block.photos}>
<a href="<{$xoops_url}>/modules/extgallery/public-photo.php?photoId=<{$photo.photo_id}
>">
    <img src="<{$xoops_url}>/uploads/extgallery/public-photo/thumb/thumb_<
{$photo.photo_name}>"
        alt="<{$photo.photo_desc}>" title="<{$photo.photo_desc}>" />
    </a>
<{/foreach}>
```

Currently, thumbnails will be displayed—but that is too small for us. Let's change it to display medium-size images:

```
<{foreach item=photo from=$block.photos}>
<a href="<{$xoops_url}>/modules/extgallery/public-photo.php?photoId=<{$photo.photo_id}
>">
    <img src="<{$xoops_url}>/uploads/extgallery/public-photo/medium/<
{$photo.photo_name}>"
        alt="<{$photo.photo_desc}>" title="<{$photo.photo_desc}>" />
</a>
<{/foreach}>
```

Integrate with the InsMinimal theme

Now open *InsMinimal/tpl/slideshow.html*. You can see that the slideshow structure is pretty simple. We don't even need to modify the structure.

Suppose you want to use the center center block to display your slideshow. First, find the following line in *theme.html*:

```
<div class="slideshow">
<{includeq file="$theme_name/slideshow.html"}>
</div>
```

Comment out the `includeq` and add the following code after that line:

```
<div class="slideshow">
<!-- <{includeq file="$theme_name/slideshow.html"}> -->
<{foreach item=block from=$xoBlocks.page_topcenter}>
        <{$block.content}>
<{/foreach}>
</div>
```

Then comment out the following code about displaying the center center block:

```
<div class="grid_3">
    <{foreach item=block from=$xoBlocks.page_topcenter}>
        <div class="block">
            <h2><{$block.title}></h2>
            <{$block.content}>
        </div>
    <{/foreach}>
</div>
```

Now you have to add the block you just modified to the home page. Go to *XOOPS backend→block management*, and enable *Random photo* block in extGallery (see Figure 6-5).

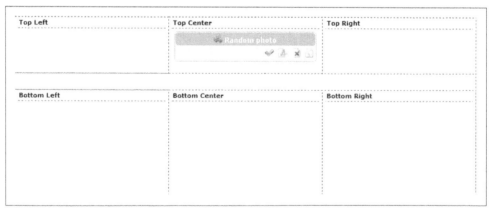

Figure 6-5. Enable the Random photo block in the center center position

Do not confuse the Random photo block with the Random photo (slideshow) block. Also, please make sure it is the only center center block!

A Test Run

Now we'll add the two photos to extGallery. But before that, let's adjust the medium photo size in *extGallery→Preferences* (see Figure 6-6).

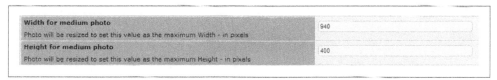

Figure 6-6. Adjusting the medium photo size in extGallery

Set the width to 940, and the height to 400. (The setting here is related to the size of your photos and the slideshow stylesheet.) Add a category, then add the two photos (Figure 6-7)—and don't forget to approve them!

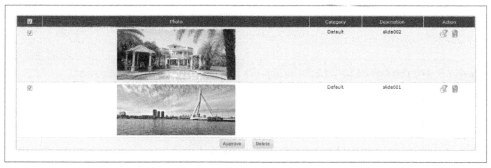

Figure 6-7. Adding the photos for our slideshow

Then, refresh the home page. Hopefully it's working! You might be skeptical: it looks the same as before. How can you prove that our method works? Let's add a third photo (see Figure 6-8).

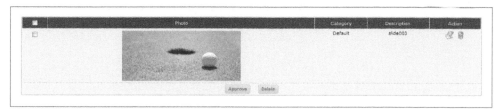

Figure 6-8. Adding a third photo to the slideshow

Refresh your home page, and the proof should now be visible, as in Figure 6-9.

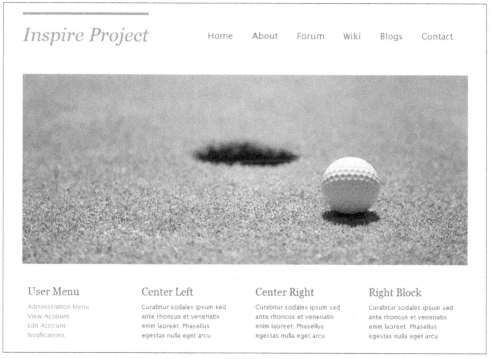

Figure 6-9. The third photo we added now appears in the slideshow on the home page

A Look Back

I hope you are not puzzled by the code here. The code is not important, but the thought process is. So let's look back and see what you've done:

- You got a theme with a hardcoded slideshow.
- You overrode the random photo block template in extGallery, so that it fit the structure of the slideshow
- You replaced the hardcoded slideshow with a center center block.
- You displayed the Random photo block in the center center block.
- You added photos in extGallery and they were displayed in the block.

CHAPTER 7

Block Anywhere Techniques

XOOPS provides you with eight block positions, which should be more than enough in most cases. However, for a very complex home page, you may still run out of blocks. And sometimes you want to totally abandon the traditional block layout for your home page, as the block layout can look quite old-fashioned.

The key question is how to fully customize your XOOPS home page, without the limitation of the block system. Well, it may sound a bit fancy and high-tech, but actually it isn't. Thanks to the work of some module developers, we have several solutions available. I've picked one that I believe is the easiest: the *XOOPS Tools module*. Of course, you can search for other solutions, but the mechanism is the same: making use of Smarty plug-ins.

How to Get XOOPS Tools Module

This module was made by developers from XOOPS China, and the file can be found in the repository there. But so you don't have to deal with Chinese characters, I have uploaded the latest version to my code forge page at *http://code.google.com/p/insraq/ downloads/list* (Figure 7-1), and you can download it there. Let me be clear that it is not my work; I cannot take credit for it. I am just illustrating how to use this great module.

Figure 7-1. You can find the XOOPS Tools module on my code forge page

After you have downloaded the package, you will find two folders in the zip archive: *modules* and *class*. Please copy those two folders to your XOOPS root folder. The *modules* folder contains the main module interface and the *class* folder contains the Smarty plug-in. Please make sure you have copied both folders.

Then install the module as usual. For the following example, I will continue to use InsMinimal theme.

A First Play-around

Now go to the *backend→XOOPS Tools→Block Callback→Add a block* (see Figure 7-2).

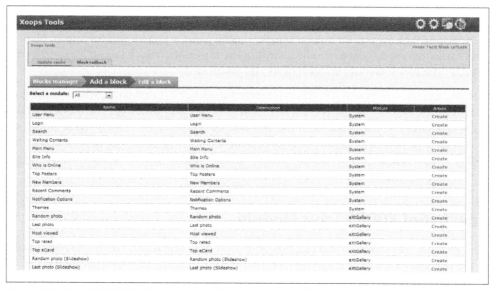

Figure 7-2. The XOOPS Tools backend will let us create new blocks

You should find all the blocks are listed here. Click the *Create* link of the *Site Info* block (see Figure 7-3).

You will be led to a page with some codes and options. The upper part—i.e., the code section—provides the code for you to display the block, while the lower part—i.e., the option section—allows you to modify the setting of the code. After modification, you'll have to resubmit and regenerate the code.

First, copy the code from the text area labeled *Simple*:

```
<{xoBlk module="system" file="system_blocks.php" show_func="b_system_info_show"
    options="320|190|s_poweredby.gif|1" template="system_block_siteinfo.html"}>
```

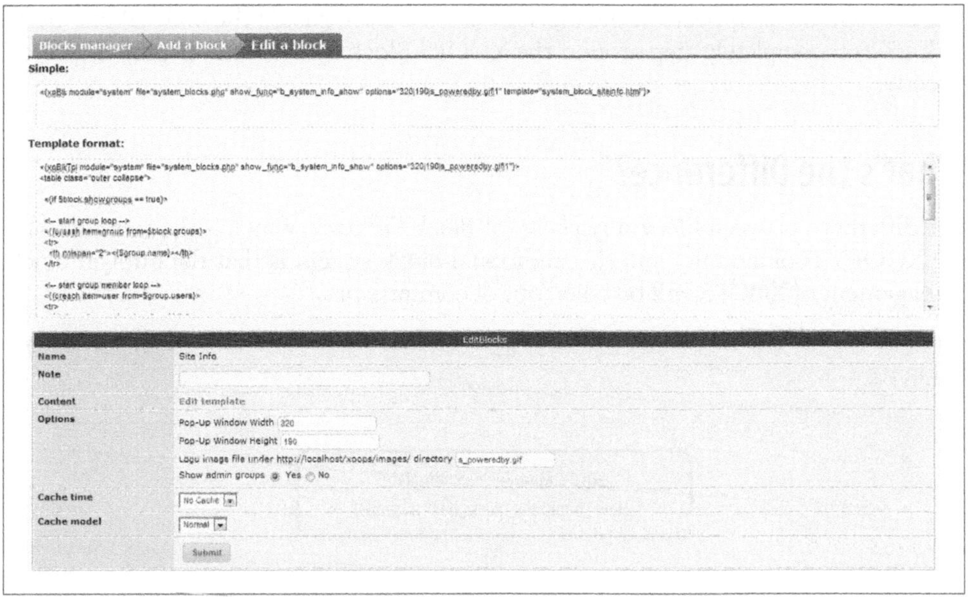

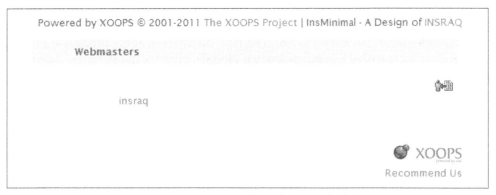

Figure 7-3. Choose the Site Info block and click the Create link

Then open go to *XOOPS/themes/InsMinimal*, open *theme.html*, and paste that code into `<div class="footer">`:

```
<div class="footer">
    <{$xoops_footer}> | InsMinimal - A Design of <a href="http://insraq.me">INSRAQ</a>
    <{xoBlk module="system" file="system_blocks.php" show_func="b_system_info_show"
        options="320|190|s_poweredby.gif|1" template="system_block_siteinfo.html"}>
</div>
```

Save the file and refresh your home page (it should look like Figure 7-4).

Figure 7-4. When you refresh the home page, you'll see the Site Info block you placed

The *Site Info* block appears in the place where you have pasted the code! Pretty neat, isn't it? You completely step around the XOOPS Block System and display the block directly.

What's the Difference?

The difference between *Block Anywhere* (or *Block Callback*, which is the term used by the XOOPS Tool module) and the traditional block system is that the built-in block management of XOOPS will be taken out of commission.

The traditional block system mechanism can be summarized with the diagram shown in Figure 7-5.

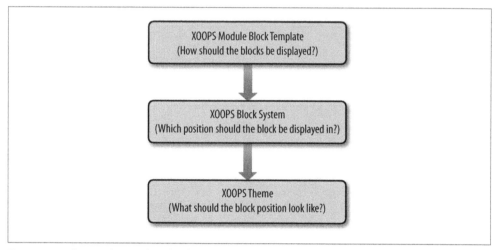

Figure 7-5. The usual procedure for displaying blocks and setting block styles in XOOPS

The *XOOPS module block template* tells us how the content of the block will be displayed. This is controlled by each individual module, but we can use the module template override technique, introduced in the previous chapter, to change the template.

The *XOOPS block system* is built-in with XOOPS; it is the most commonly used block management system. It provides eight block positions by default. The block system determines which block should be displayed in which position. For example, the *Latest News* block from the News module should be displayed in the center center position.

As for the *XOOPS theme*, it determines what the block should look like. The name of the block is just a convention: left block does not have to be placed on the left. Actually, you can put it on the right, but that would be very misleading. Consider the slideshow example in the previous chapter, wherein the center center block became the slideshow. The traditional 8-block-position system can really be viewed as a communication channel.

By using Block Anywhere techniques, we use the *XOOPS Tools* module to replace the original communication channel, so the diagram looks like Figure 7-6 instead.

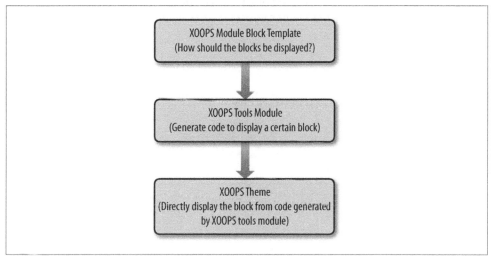

Figure 7-6. The procedure for using the Block Anywhere technique to display custom blocks in XOOPS

This way, the 8-block-position limitation is avoided: you can display any block in your theme, and there is no limitation on the number of blocks. Sounds good, doesn't it? Then why not abolish the traditional block system and replace it with XOOPS Tools?

The consideration here is generality of themes. The 8-block-position system is built in with every XOOPS installation. If you, as a designer, follow the conventions, your theme should work on every XOOPS installation.

Using the 8-block-position system in website A, you could display the center center block in `<div class="content">` and the right block in `<div class="sidebar">`; in the center center block, you could choose to display *Latest News*, and in the right block, display *Latest Photos*. Then in website B, if you applied the same theme, you could display *Latest Forum Topics* in the center center block and *Latest Comments* in the right block. It wouldn't matter which module you chose: the theme only specifies the positions, not individual module templates.

However, XOOPS Tools is website-specific. If in website A, you displayed *Latest News* in `<div class="content">` and *Latest Photos* in `<div class="sidebar">`, and then applied the theme to website B, you would have to install the same modules on both websites and you could *only* display *Latest News* in `<div class="content">` and *Latest Photos* in `<div class="sidebar">`. Clearly, this largely limits the flexibility of themes.

This chapter has been a bit theoretical. I know you probably don't like theories—neither do I. But to actually take advantage of this technique, you have to build a complex home page with lots of customized blocks. In the next chapter, I will use a complete case study example to illustrate Block Anywhere, as well as aggregate other techniques introduced in this book.

CHAPTER 8

Case Study: My TinyMag

Wireframing

Let's begin by visualizing the layout. Wireframing tools are very useful. I personally prefer Pencil, which is a Firefox extension as well as a standalone product (*http://pencil.evolus.vn/*). Using it, I've designed quite a complex home page structure, shown in Figure 8-1. (Note that it is only for illustration purposes: please don't judge the design according to UI or UX principles!)

When making prototypes, start by thinking about which modules you are going to use. For an article module, I chose Publisher. It's based on SmartSection and was developed by Trabis. Although it is only in alpha, it is already quite stable. However, since the author hasn't provided the latest version for download, you'll have to check it out from his code forge at *http://code.google.com/p/xuups/source/browse/trunk/modules/*.

 If using SVN is painful for you, you can use the Publisher version I checked out on February 9, 2011, at *http://code.google.com/p/insraq/downloads/list*. It works well on my XOOPS 2.5 installation. See Figure 8-2.

For building polls, I chose the XOOPSPoll module. You can get it from the official module repository at *http://xoops.org/modules/repository/singlefile.php?cid=51&lid=1897*.

For a forum module, I chose CBB 4.03 by Alfred. You can download the latest version from his SVN repository at *http://svn.myxoops.org/*, and you don't need to do a SVN check-out. Remember to rename the module folder *newbb*.

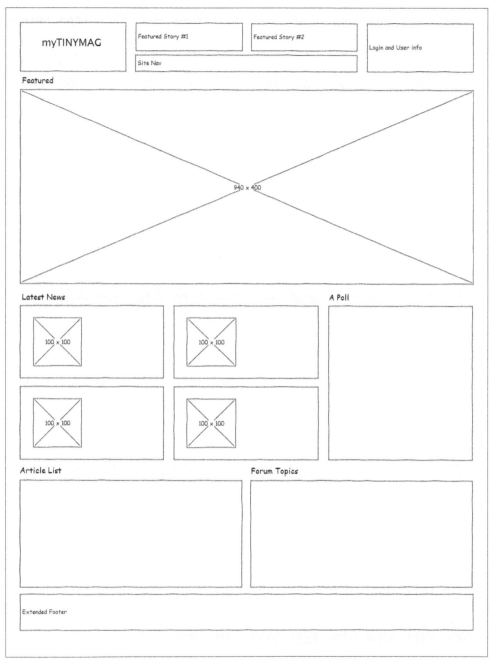

Figure 8-1. A wireframe of the home page we will build in this chapter

Figure 8-2. A version of Publisher checked out on February 9, 2011 is available for download if you prefer to avoid Subversion

Mock Up a Design

This step is basically the same as with other design jobs. Open your favorite graphic editor—Photoshop, Fireworks, or GIMP—and choose a nice color scheme, make several graphics, and pick a typography set.

Here I've used the 960 Grid System to assist me in the design process. It is widely used and easier to apply to XOOPS. We will look at it more closely in the next section.

Actually, to code the design mock-up shown in Figure 8-3, the traditional 8-block-position system is more than adequate. However, I've intentionally tried to use Block Anywhere techniques here.

Code the Mock-Up Design

The traditional method is to first code in XHTML and CSS, and then integrate the template into XOOPS. Luckily, we will be using the 960 Grid System (Figure 8-4), which I have adapted to XOOPS. You can download it from my code forge at *http://code.google.com/p/insraq/downloads/list*.

Now unzip the folder in *XOOPS/themes/*, and rename it from *960* to *mytinymag*.

Header

Open *theme.html* and code the `<!-- header -->` section as follows:

```
theme.html (excerpt)
<!--- Header -->
<div class="container_12">
    <div class="grid_10">
    <div class="grid_4 alpha"><a href="<{xoAppUrl}>">
        <img src="<{xoImgUrl}>img/logo.png"
        alt="<{$xoops_sitename}>" /></a>
    </div>
    <div class="grid_3">
        <div class="header-feature">
        <a href="#">
            <img src="<{xoImgUrl img/feature_1.png}>"
            alt="Feature 1" />
        </a>
```

Figure 8-3. The mock-up design includes featured articles, latest articles, a poll, an archive, and a forum

Figure 8-4. The 960 Grid System available for download

```
            <span class="title ptsans">
                Best place to go for holiday
            </span>
        </div>
    </div>
<div class="grid_3 omega">
    <div class="header-feature">
        <a href="#">
            <img src="<{xoImgUrl img/feature_2.png}>"
            alt="Feature 2" />
        </a>          <span class="title ptsans">
            Know more about you DC
        </span>
    </div>
</div>
<div class="clear"></div>
<div class="grid_4 alpha">
    <p class="slogan ptsans">
        Tiny magazine,big world!
    </p>
</div>
<div class="grid_6 omega">
    <ul class="nav">
        <li><a href="#">Home</a></li>
        <li><a href="#">Travel</a></li>
        <li><a href="#">Digital</a></li>
        <li><a href="#">Food</a></li>
        <li><a href="#">Sports</a></li>
        <li><a href="#">Forum</a></li>
    </ul>
</div>
<div class="clear"></div>
    </div>
    <div class="grid_2">
        <a href="<{xoAppUrl user.php}>" class="header-login">Login</a>
        <a href="<{xoAppUrl register.php}>" class="header-register">Register</a>
    </div>
    <div class="clear"></div>
</div>
<div class="sep-20"></div>
```

My folder structure is shown in Figure 8-5.

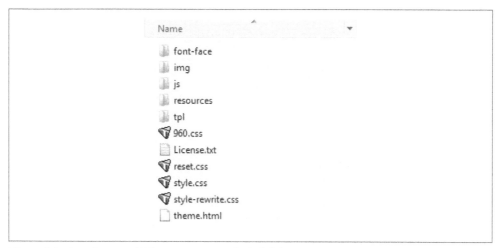

Figure 8-5. A peek at my folder structure may be helpful

Giving the image source as `<{xoImgUrl img/feature_1.png}>` indicates that the image is placed in the *img* folder. If you type that in, XOOPS will automatically locate the resources.

Here is the related stylesheet:

style.css (excerpt)
```
/* Theme Specific Style */

.ptsans {
    font-family: 'PTSansRegular', Arial, Verdana, sans-serif;
}

.sep-20 {
    margin: 10px 0;
}

.sep-30 {
    margin: 15px 0;
}

.sep-40 {
    margin: 20px 0;
}

/* Header */

.header-feature {
    position: relative;
}

.header-feature .title {
    position: absolute;
    top: 0;
```

```
        left: 0;
        width: 220px;
        color: #fff;
        background: url(img/70.png);
        font-size: 16px;
        text-align: center;
}

.header-feature .title a, .header-feature .title a:hover {
        color: #fff;
}

.header-login, .header-register {
        display: block;
        width: 140px;
        padding: 15px 0;
        color: #fff;
        text-align: center;
        font-family: 'PTSansBold', Arial, Verdana, sans-serif;
        font-size: 16px;
}

.header-login:hover, .header-register:hover {
        color: #fff;
}

.header-login {
        background: #ccc;
}

.header-register {
        background: #9BBCDD;
        margin: 5px 0 0 0;
}

.slogan {
        text-align: right;
        margin: 0 10px 0 0;
        color: #999;
        font-size: 20px;
}

ul.nav {
        font-size: 20px;
        font-family: 'PTSansBold', Arial, Verdana, sans-serif;
}

ul.nav a {
        color: #666;
}

ul.nav a:hover {
        color: #333;
        border-bottom: 3px solid #6699CC;
}
```

```
ul.nav li {
    float: left;
    margin: 0 20px 0 0;
}
```

I used the font PT-Sans, which can be acquired from FontSquirrel (*http://www.fonts quirrel.com/fonts/PT-Sans*).

How to Deal with Content

Now let's stop for a minute and think about how we will approach the content:

Home page
    Completely abandon block system, use Block Anywhere technique

Other pages
    Two-column layout, display module content and right block

Here is the problem: XOOPS does not provide an `<{if $homepage}>` function, so how will it know whether we are working on the home page or not?

You could hack the XOOPS core to fix this, but that would cause trouble when it comes time to upgrade later on. Instead, the best practice is to make use of the original block system. Display a customized HTML block in the center center position and set it to display only on "top page." Then you can use `<{if $xoBlocks.page_topcenter}>` to judge whether a given page is a home page or not. The customized HTML block will not be displayed if you do not call the `foreach` loop to display it.

So the structure for content will look like this:

```
<{if $xoBlocks.page_topcenter}>
            <!-- Here goes the code of customized home page -->
<{else}>
            <!-- Module content -->
            <!-- Right block -->
<{/if}>
```

The actual code looks like this:

```
theme.html (excerpt)
<div class="container_12">
    <!-- if home page -->
    <{if $xoBlocks.page_topcenter}>
        <!-- Customized home page -->
        <!-- if not home page -->
    <{else}>
        <!-- Module content -->
        <{if $xoops_contents && ($xoops_contents != '') }>
            <div class="grid_9">
                <{$xoops_contents}>
            </div>
        <{/if}>
```

```
        <{if $xoBlocks.canvas_right}>
            <!-- Right Blocks -->
            <div class="grid_3">
                <{foreach item=block from=$xoBlocks.canvas_right}>
                    <div class="right-block-content">
                            <h2><{$block.title}></h2>
                            <{$block.content}>
                    </div>
                <{/foreach}>
            </div>
        <{/if}>
    <{/if}>
    <div class="clear"></div>
</div>
```

Make sure you understand why we are doing this. If you feel comfortable, then let's move on.

Content Markup

Create the markup and stylesheet for featured content:

```
theme.html (excerpt)
<!-- Content -->
<div class="container_12">
    <!-- if home page -->
    <{if $xoBlocks.page_topcenter}>
        <!-- Featured content -->
        <div class="grid_12 content-feature">
            <img src="<{xoImgUrl img/slideshow_940_400.png}>" alt="" />
            <div class="title">Featured: WOW! The bridge</div>
            <div class="grid_10 alpha">
                <p>
                    Lorem ipsum dolor sit amet, consectetur
                    adipiscing elit. Donec suscipit odio sed libero feugiat
                    dignissim. Praesent mollis, sapien vel vulputate imperdiet,
                    consectetur adipiscing elit.
                </p>
            </div>
            <div class="grid_2 omega read-more"><a href="#">Read More</a></div>
        </div>
        <div class="clear"></div>
        <div class="sep-20"></div>
        <!-- Latest Articles -->
        <div class="grid_8">
            <h2 class="title">Latest Articles</h2>
            <div class="grid_4 alpha">
                <div class="content-article">
                    <h3 class="title">
                        Travel: A Good Place for Winter
                    </h3>
                    <a href="#">
                        <img src="<{xoImgUrl img/art_img_1.png}>" alt="" />
                    </a>
```

```
            <p>
                Morbi ac tellus sed metus vestibulum, morbi ac
                tellus sed metus vestibulum, orbi ac tellus sed
                metus vestibulum
            </p>
        </div>
    </div>
    <div class="grid_4 omega">
        <div class="content-article">
            <h3 class="title">
                Digital: The Latest DC is On!
            </h3>
            <a href="#">
                <img src="<{xoImgUrl img/art_img_2.png}>" alt="" />
            </a>
            <p>
                Morbi ac tellus sed metus vestibulum, morbi ac
                tellus sed metus vestibulum, orbi ac tellus sed
                metus vestibulum
            </p>
        </div>
    </div>
    <div class="clear"></div>
    <div class="sep-20"></div>
    <div class="grid_4 alpha">
        <div class="content-article">
            <h3 class="title">
                Food: Know More About Lobster
            </h3>
            <a href="#">
                <img src="<{xoImgUrl img/art_img_3.png}>" alt="" />
            </a>
            <p>
                Morbi ac tellus sed metus vestibulum, morbi ac
                tellus sed metus vestibulum, orbi ac tellus sed
                metus vestibulum
            </p>
        </div>
    </div>
    <div class="grid_4 omega">
        <div class="content-article">
            <h3 class="title">
                Sports: Teach Yourself Golf!</h3>
             </h3>
            <a href="#">
                <img src="<{xoImgUrl img/art_img_3.png}>" alt="" />
            </a>
            <p>
                Morbi ac tellus sed metus vestibulum, morbi ac
                tellus sed metus vestibulum, orbi ac tellus sed
                metus vestibulum
            </p>
        </div>
    </div>
</div>
```

```
<div class="grid_4">
    <h2 class="title lighter">What do you think?</h2>
    <div class="content-general">
        <p>Placeholder for XOOPS Poll</p>
    </div>
</div>
<div class="clear"></div>
<div class="sep-20"></div>
<div class="grid_6">
    <h2 class="title">Archives</h2>
    <div class="content-general">
        <p>Placeholder for Archives</p>
    </div>
</div>
<div class="grid_6">
    <h2 class="title">Discussions</h2>
    <div class="content-general">
        <p>Placeholder for Forum Topics</p>
    </div>
</div>
<!-- if not home page -->
<{else}>
    <!-- Module content -->
    <{if $xoops_contents && ($xoops_contents != '') }>
        <div class="grid_9">
            <div class="content-general"><{$xoops_contents}></div>
        </div>
    <{/if}>
    <{if $xoBlocks.canvas_right}>
        <!-- Right Blocks -->
        <div class="grid_3">
            <div class="content-general">
            <{foreach item=block from=$xoBlocks.canvas_right}>
                <div class="right-block-content">
                    <h2><{$block.title}></h2>
                    <{$block.content}>
                </div>
            <{/foreach}>
            </div>
        </div>
    <{/if}>
<{/if}>
<div class="clear"></div>
</div>
<div class="sep-40"></div>
<div class="container_12">
    <div class="grid_12">
        <div class="content-general footer"><{$xoops_footer}></div>
    </div>
    <div class="clear"></div>
</div>
<div class="sep-20"></div>
```

style.css (excerpt)
```css
/* Featured Content */

.content-feature {
    border-bottom: 1px solid #ddd;
    position: relative;
}

.content-feature p {
    margin: 5px 0;
}

.content-feature .title a {
    position: absolute;
    padding: 15px;
    right: 0;
    top: 0;
    background: url(img/70.png);
    color: #fff;
    font-family: 'PTSansRegular', Arial, Verdana, sans-serif;
    font-size: 20px;
}

.content-feature .title a:hover {
    color: #fff;
}

.read-more a {
    background: #99CC00;
    display: block;
    margin: 5px 0;
    padding: 10px 0;
    text-align: center;
    color: #fff;
    font-size: 18px;
    font-family: 'PTSansBold', Arial, Verdana, sans-serif;
}

.read-more a:hover {
    color: #fff;
}

/* Content */

h2.title {
    font-size: 30px;
    color: #333;
    font-family: 'PTSansRegular', Arial, Verdana, sans-serif;
}

h2.lighter {
    color: #999;
}
```

```css
.content-article {
    border: 1px solid #ddd;
}

.content-article:hover {
    border: 1px solid #ccc;
}

.content-article img {
    width: 298px;
    height: auto;
}

.content-article p {
    padding: 10px;
}

h3.title {
    font-size: 18px;
    font-family: Georgia, "Times New Roman", Times, serif;
    font-style: italic;
    text-align: center;
    margin: 10px 0;
}

.content-general {
    border: 1px solid #ddd;
    padding: 10px;
}

.content-general:hover {
    border: 1px solid #ccc;
}

/* Footer */

.footer {
    text-align: center;
}
```

The above code is probably a piece of cake for you design champs, so I don't need to explain it. But I have to say a few words about why we didn't code Poll, Archives, or Discussions blocks.

The module itself has some block templates. In some places, we can just modify these templates instead of completely rewriting them. But in other places, the module templates won't fit at all, so we have to rewrite the templates—and it doesn't really matter in which step we do this.

The image files in the *img* folder will be as shown in Figure 8-6.

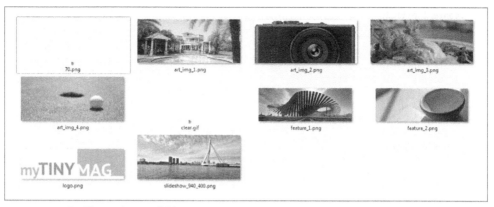

Figure 8-6. The files in the img folder

Refresh your browser and you should see something similar to the screenshot shown in Figure 8-7.

Set Up Blocks

Before we apply the Block Anywhere technique, we will first need to set up blocks. Add a Center Center Control Block, as shown in Figure 8-8.

Make sure the blocks we want to display are as shown in Figure 8-9: Center Center Control Block should appear under Top Center; and Main Menu, Themes, and User Menu should appear on the Right.

Publisher FAQ

Before you actually apply the Block Anywhere technique, let's play around with Publisher first. Publisher's backend is quite user-friendly, but there are a few places where you need to pay special attention.

Where are the advanced editing options?

Publisher has lots of advanced editing options, including article image upload, which you will probably use quite often. But after installing the module, you'll see the basic interface as shown in Figure 8-10.

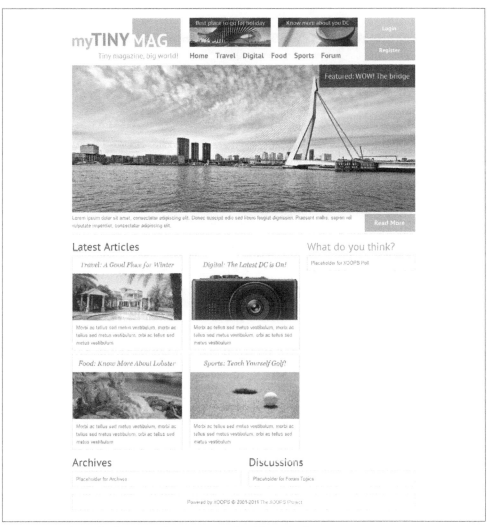

Figure 8-7. After refreshing your browser, you should see this layout

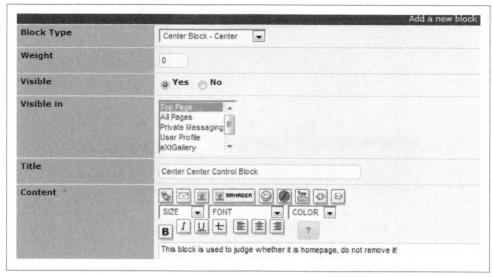

Figure 8-8. Adding a Center Center Control Block

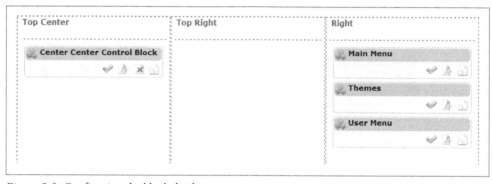

Figure 8-9. Configuring the block display

Figure 8-10. The basic Publisher interface; to access the advanced options, change the default Permissions settings

The trick here is setting permissions: by default, you do not have permission to use the advanced options, but you can grant yourself permission in the *Permissions* tab (see Figure 8-11).

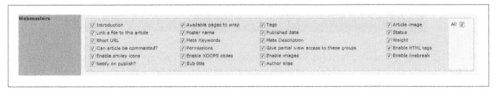

Figure 8-11. Go ahead and grant yourself full permissions

After changing the settings, you will be able to see the full edit options, as shown in Figure 8-12.

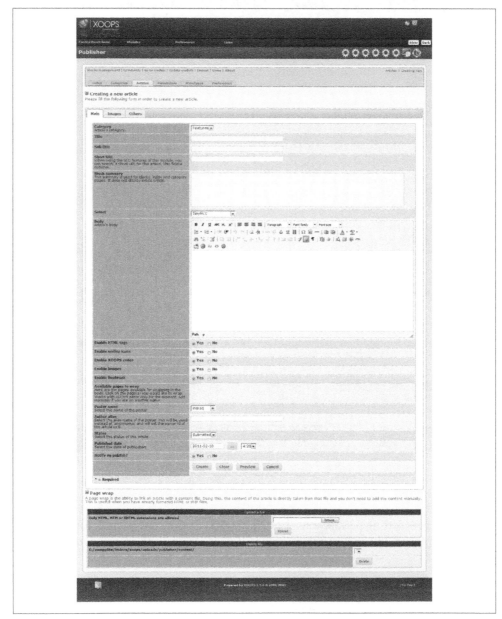

Figure 8-12. After granting yourself additional permissions, you'll see more options in the Publisher interface

And there are two more tabs: *Images* and *Others*.

Why can't I upload article images?

Publisher makes use of the built-in XOOPS image manager (access this by going to *Modules→System→Image Manager*, as shown in Figure 8-13). You first need to add at least one category.

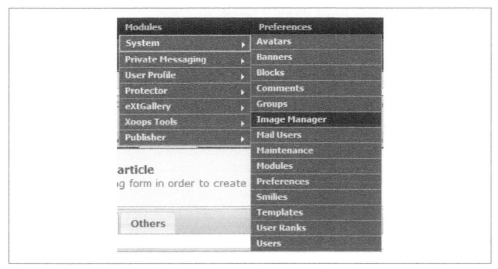

Figure 8-13. Use the Image Manager to add image categories

When adding categories, pay attention to the permission settings and the maximum width, maximum height, and maximum file size—the default settings might not be suitable (see Figure 8-14). For example, the default maximum file size is only 50KB, which is obviously too small.

After adjusting the settings, you should be able to upload article images in Publisher.

For the purposes of this case study, please create an image category for each article category to keep things neat and tidy. The categories in Publisher and the corresponding categories in Image Manager are shown in Figures 8-15 and 8-16.

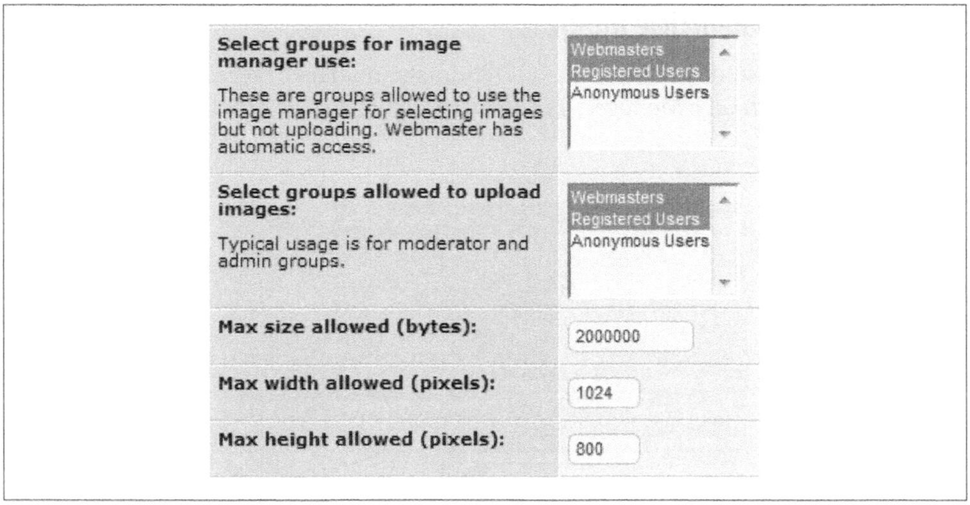

Figure 8-14. You may need to adjust the default image settings

Figure 8-15. These are the article categories we are using in Publisher

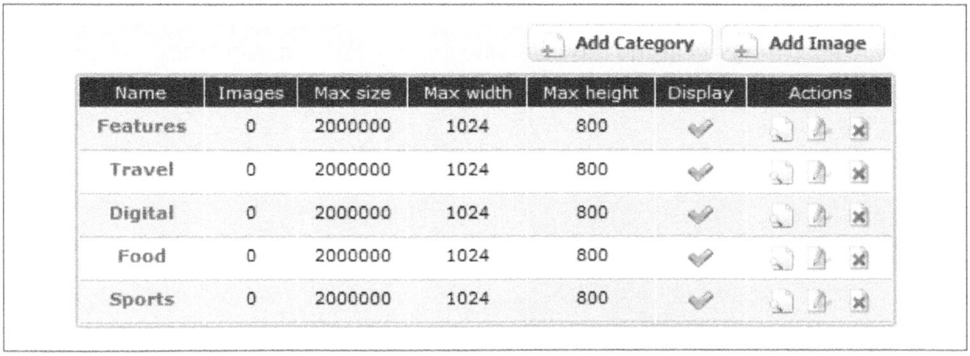

Figure 8-16. Create image categories in Image Manager that correspond to the article categories in Publisher

Construct Header Feature

Go to the XOOPS Tools module, choose *Add a block*, and add *Latest News* from the Publisher module.

You will see lots of options, but what you need to adjust are the following:

- Exclude first: 1
- Display: 1
- Show Article Image: Yes
- Image Width: 220
- Image Height: 78

The first and second of these ensure that the *second latest* article or feature will show, because we want to display the latest in the large feature style. The final two options solely affect the design. You can upload a large image and Publisher will display the thumbnail. Click *Submit*.

You may notice that there are two sets of code, as shown in Figure 8-17: the one named *Simple* uses the default template, while the one called *Template format* allows you to modify the template directly. Of course, we will use the latter.

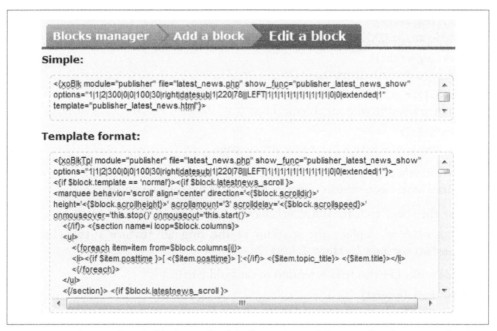

Figure 8-17. The Simple code block sets the default template, while "Template format" code allows you to modify the template

You'll see a lot of <{if}> clauses—those are for those display options. We just need the following code:

```
tpl/feature_1.html
<{xoBlkTpl module="publisher" file="latest_news.php"
    show_func="publisher_latest_news_show"
    options="1|1|2|300|0|0|100|30|right|datesub|1|220|78|||LEFT
    |1|1|1|1|1|1|1|1|1|0|0|extended|1"}>
<{section name=i}>
    <div class="header-feature">
        <{foreach item=item from=$block.columns[i]}>
            <a href="<{$item.itemurl}>">
                <img src="<{$item.item_image}>"
                height="<{$block.imgheight}>"
                title="<{$item.alt}>" alt="<{$item.alt}>" />
            </a>
            <span class="title ptsans"><{$item.title}></span>
        <{/foreach}>
    </div>
<{/section}>
<{/xoBlkTpl}>
```

I have already adapted this code to the design. Here are some explanations of the Smarty variables:

<{$item.itemurl}>
> Links to the article

<{$item.item_image}>
> Article image URL

<{$block.imgheight}>
> The height of article image

<{$item.alt}>
> Usually, the title without any markup

<{$item.title}>
> The article title with a link to the article page

You can directly copy and paste the code to replace the original markup, but to make *theme.html* look nicer, we can organize the files in the following way:

1. Save the above code to *XOOPS/themes/mytinymag/tpl/feature_1.html*.

2. In *theme.html*, replace the markup of the original feature_1 to <{includeq file="$theme_name/feature_1.html"}>.

The code looks like this (pay attention to the bold part):

```
theme.html (excerpt)
<!--- Header -->
<div class="container_12">
    <div class="grid_10">
```

```
<div class="grid_4 alpha">
    <a href="<{xoAppUrl}>">
    <img src="<{xoImgUrl img/logo.png}>"
    alt="<{$xoops_sitename}>" />
    </a>
</div>
<div class="grid_3">
    <{includeq file="$theme_name/feature_1.html"}>
</div>
```

What about the second feature? You could start from 0 and repeat all the steps. But reusing what we've already done seems better.

The second feature will display the third-latest featured article. The only difference from feature_1 is the *Exclude first* option: we should set it to **2**.

Now look at the code in *tpl/feature_1.html*, and you will see a series of numbers in the first line:

```
<{xoBlkTpl module-"publisher" file="latest_news.php"
    show_func="publisher_latest_news_show"
    options="1|1|2|300|0|0|100|30|right|datesub|1|220|78|||LEFT
    |1|1|1|1|1|1|1|1|1|0|0|extended|1"}>
```

Those numbers are not meaningless; they record the options for the block. And they are presented in the same order as on the *Edit a block* page. What you need to do is change the first **1** to **2**:

```
<{xoBlkTpl module-"publisher" file="latest_news.php"
    show_func="publisher_latest_news_show"
    options="2|1|2|300|0|0|100|30|right|datesub|1|220|78|||LEFT
    |1|1|1|1|1|1|1|1|1|0|0|extended|1"}>
```

Save a copy as *feature_2.html*, and replace the original markup with an includeq clause:

```
theme.html (excerpt)
<!--- Header -->
<div class="container_12">
    <div class="grid_10">
        <div class="grid_4 alpha">
            <a href="<{xoAppUrl}>">
            <img src="<{xoImgUrl img/logo.png}>"
            alt="<{$xoops_sitename}>" />
            </a>
        </div>
        <div class="grid_3">
            <{includeq file="$theme_name/feature_1.html"}>
        </div>
        <div class="grid_3 omega">
            <{includeq file="$theme_name/feature_2.html"}>
        </div>
        <div class="clear"></div>
```

Construct the Main Feature

Save *feature_1.html* as *feature_main.html*, and change the first parameter from 1 to 0 so that it will display the latest article. The fourth parameter tells XOOPS how many words to display; set it to 200 to fit your design. Finally, adjust the image size by changing 220 to 940, and 78 to 400.

```
<{xoBlkTpl module="publisher" file="latest_news.php"
    show_func="publisher_latest_news_show"
    options="0|1|2|200|0|0|100|30|right|datesub|1|940|400|||LEFT
    |1|1|1|1|1|1|1|1|1|1|0|0|extended|1"}>
```

Once you are familiar with the syntax, you won't even need to go to the XOOPS Tools module: you can directly modify the parameters.

Adapt it to our design:

```
<{xoBlkTpl module="publisher" file="latest_news.php"
    show_func="publisher_latest_news_show"
    options="0|1|2|200|0|0|100|30|right|datesub|1|940|400|||LEFT
    |1|1|1|1|1|1|1|1|1|1|0|0|extended|1"}>
<{section name=i}>
        <{foreach item=item from=$block.columns[i]}>
            <img src="<{$item.item_image}>" height="<{$block.imgheight}>"
                title="<{$item.alt}>" alt="<{$item.alt}>" />
            <div class="title"><{$item.title}></div>
            <div class="grid_10 alpha"><p><{$item.text}></p></div>
            <div class="grid_2 omega read-more"><{$item.more}></div>
        <{/foreach}>
<{/section}>
<{/xoBlkTpl}>
```

Here is an explanation of Smarty variables:

`<{$item.text}>`
:   The first 200 words of the article, which we set in options

`<{$item.more}>`
:   A "Read more..." that links to the article page

You might be wondering how we figure out the meaning of the Smarty variables. One way is by guessing, as the names of the variables are often self-explanatory. Another way is trial and error: you can place different variables in the template and find out how they affect the display.

Now do the markup replacement:

```
<!-- Featured content -->
<div class="grid_12 content-feature">
    <{includeq file="$theme_name/feature_main.html"}>
</div>
```

Construct the Content

Let's post the three sample articles (see Figure 8-18). The latest one should use an article image size of 940×400, while the next two should be 220×78.

ID	Category	Title	Created	Action
5	Features	WOW! The bridge	2011/2/10	
2	Features	Best place to go for holiday	2011/2/9	
1	Features	Know more about your DC	2011/2/9	

Figure 8-18. Queuing up our three sample articles

In case you do not know how to add an article image, let's go through it together. When adding a new article:

1. Click the *Images* tab, choose the proper category, and type in a description.
2. Click *Upload new image* and choose the file you want to upload.
3. If the upload is successful, the image name should appear on the righthand list, and will also be displayed in the *Image preview* section (see Figure 8-19).

You can also choose an existing image from the list on the left and click *Add* to append it to the article.

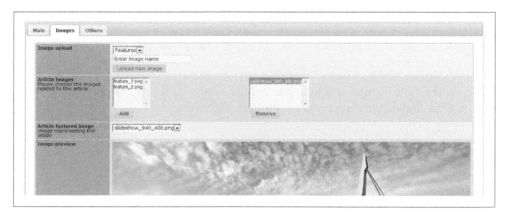

Figure 8-19. Adding a new article image

Actually, the correct way to do this is to upload a full-size article image for *all* articles and let Publisher control the display size by changing the image-size options for the block. Here, for simplicity, I directly uploaded image thumbnails for featured articles in the header, and a full-size image for the main featured article.

 You might have noticed that the thumbnails and large images are not proportional. In practice, you should make sure that they *are* proportional—take this into consideration when you do the mock-up design. However, since the design here is only for illustration purposes, I've simply ignored those analytical procedures.

Refresh your browser to see the result shown in Figure 8-20.

Figure 8-20. The home page now features a full-size main article image, and two thumbnail-size article images

Click on the first feature article in the header, and you'll see that the article page (Figure 8-21) looks pretty nice even without further work!

Figure 8-21. The feature article page after clicking through from the home page

Construct Latest Article Categories

Constructing the *Latest Article* part won't be too difficult if you understood the previous section. Here, I'll just go through the code and highlight the parts to which you need to pay special attention:

tpl/latest_travel.html

```
<{xoBlkTpl module="publisher" file="latest_news.php"
    show_func="publisher_latest_news_show"
```

```
    options="0|1|2|100|0|0|100|30|right|datesub|1|300|128|||LEFT
    |1|1|1|1|1|1|1|1|1|1|0|0|extended|2"}>
<{section name=i}>
    <div class="content-article">
        <{foreach item=item from=$block.columns[i]}>
            <h3 class="title">
                <a href="<{$item.itemurl}>"><{$item.alt}></a>
            </h3>
            <a href="<{$item.itemurl}>">
                <img src="<{$item.item_image}>"
                height="<{$block.imgheight}>" title="<{$item.alt}>"
                alt="<{$item.alt}>" />
            </a>
            <p><{$item.text}></p>
        <{/foreach}>
    </div>
<{/section}>
<{/xoBlkTpl}>
```

We can set an options parameter to tell XOOPS which topics to display. As the list in Figure 8-22 suggests, 0 is "All categories," 1 is "Features," 2 is "Travel," and so on. You'll need to change this parameter for each different category:

Figure 8-22. A list of topics to display corresponds to an option parameter

tpl/latest_digital.html
```
<{xoBlkTpl module="publisher" file="latest_news.php"
    show_func="publisher_latest_news_show"
    options="0|1|2|100|0|0|100|30|right|datesub|1|300|128|||LEFT
    |1|1|1|1|1|1|1|1|1|1|0|0|extended|3"}>
<{section name=i}>
<div class="content-article">
        <{foreach item=item from=$block.columns[i]}>
            <h3 class="title">
                <a href="<{$item.itemurl}>"><{$item.alt}></a>
            </h3>
            <a href="<{$item.itemurl}>">
                <img src="<{$item.item_image}>"
                height="<{$block.imgheight}>" title="<{$item.alt}>"
                alt="<{$item.alt}>" />
            </a>
            <p><{$item.text}></p>
        <{/foreach}>
```

```
        </div>
    <{/section}>
    <{/xoBlkTpl}>
```

tpl/latest_food.html
```
<{xoBlkTpl module="publisher" file="latest_news.php"
    show_func="publisher_latest_news_show"
    options="0|1|2|100|0|0|100|30|right|datesub|1|300|128|||LEFT
    |1|1|1|1|1|1|1|1|1|0|0|extended|4"}>
<{section name=i}>
    <div class="content-article">
        <{foreach item=item from=$block.columns[i]}>
            <h3 class="title">
                <a href="<{$item.itemurl}>"><{$item.alt}></a>
            </h3>
            <a href="<{$item.itemurl}>">
                <img src="<{$item.item_image}>">
                height="<{$block.imgheight}>" title="<{$item.alt}>"
                alt="<{$item.alt}>" />
            </a>
            <p><{$item.text}></p>
        <{/foreach}>
    </div>
    <{/section}>
    <{/xoBlkTpl}>
```

tpl/latest_sports.html
```
<{xoBlkTpl module="publisher" file="latest_news.php"
    show_func="publisher_latest_news_show"
    options="0|1|2|100|0|0|100|30|right|datesub|1|300|128|||LEFT
    |1|1|1|1|1|1|1|1|1|0|0|extended|5"}>
<{section name=i}>
    <div class="content-article">
        <{foreach item=item from=$block.columns[i]}>
            <h3 class="title">
                <a href="<{$item.itemurl}>"><{$item.alt}></a>
            </h3>
            <a href="<{$item.itemurl}>">
                <img src="<{$item.item_image}>">
                height="<{$block.imgheight}>" title="<{$item.alt}>"
                alt="<{$item.alt}>" />
            </a>
            <p><{$item.text}></p>
        <{/foreach}>
    </div>
    <{/section}>
    <{/xoBlkTpl}>
```

theme.html
```
<!-- Latest Articles -->
<div class="grid_8">
    <h2 class="title">Latest Articles</h2>
    <div class="grid_4 alpha">
        <{includeq file="$theme_name/latest_travel.html"}>
    </div>
```

```
<div class="grid_4 omega">
        <{includeq file="$theme_name/latest_digital.html"}>
</div>
<div class="clear"></div>
<div class="sep-20"></div>
<div class="grid_4 alpha">
        <{includeq file="$theme_name/latest_food.html"}>
</div>
<div class="grid_4 omega">
        <{includeq file="$theme_name/latest_sports.html"}>
</div>
</div>
```

Add one article in each category, using 300×128 as the article image size. Then refresh your browser (see Figure 8-23). You should see it working!

Figure 8-23. Our latest articles in different categories

Poll

Install the XOOPS Poll module via the usual method, and then generate code with the XOOPS Tools module (see Figure 8-24).

Let's try *Simple* code first (which, remember, uses the default template). Paste the code where the *Placeholder for XOOPS Poll* text appears:

```
<{xoBlk module="xoopspoll" file="xoopspoll.php" show_func="b_xoopspoll_show"
    template="xoopspoll_block_poll.html"}>
```

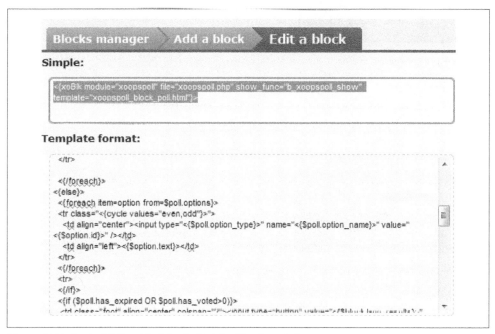

Figure 8-24. In the "Edit a block" tab, find the Simple code box

Create a poll (for this exercise, it doesn't matter too much what it is) and refresh your browser (see Figure 8-25). That looks nice! The default template actually works pretty well.

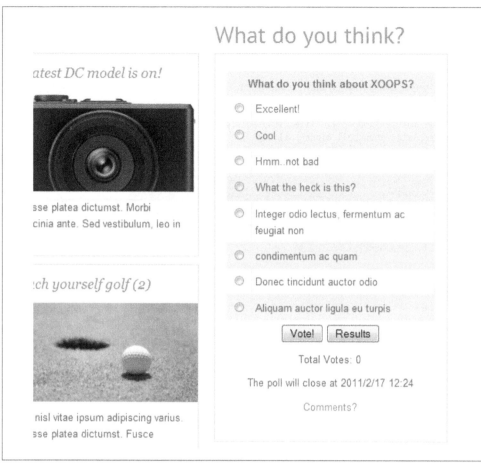

Figure 8-25. I created a dummy poll using the XOOPS Poll module

Archives and Discussions

The archives and discussions used here are from Publisher and Forum, respectively. However, they may not be suitable for our purposes, so let's tweak the code.

Archives

For Archives, let's use the *Recent Items List* block template from Publisher. First try the default template, shown in Figure 8-26.

Figure 8-26. Publisher's default template for recent items

The overall style is fine, but it looks kind of funny to have the author on a second line, so let's make a small modification to the original template:

tpl/archives.html
```
<{xoBlkTpl module="publisher" file="items_new.php"
show_func="publisher_items_new_show"
options="0|datesub|1|5|65|none"}>
    <table cellpadding="0" cellspacing="0" border="0">
    <{foreach item=newitems from=$block.newitems}>
        <tr class="<{cycle values="even,odd"}>">
        <{if $newitems.image}>
            <td>
                <img style="padding:1px;margin:2px;border:1px solid #c3c3c3"
                width="50" src="<{$newitems.image}>" title="<{$newitems.image_name}>"
                alt="<{$newitems.image_name}>" />
            </td>
        <{/if}>
        <td>
            <strong><{$newitems.link}></strong> by <{$newitems.poster}>
            <{if $block.show_order == '1'}> (<{$newitems.new}>) <{/if}>
        </td>
        </tr>
    <{/foreach}>
    </table>
    <p style="text-align: right;"><a href="modules/publisher/">All articles</a></p>
<{/xoBlkTpl}>
```

Save this as *tpl/archives.html* and include it in your *theme.html* file.

The archives should look something like Figure 8-27. Much better now!

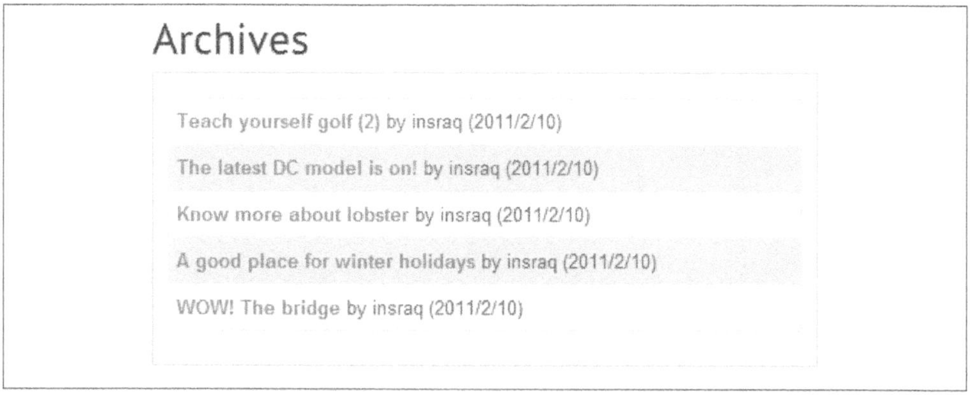

Figure 8-27. We modified the template to display the title and author all on one line

Forum

To create a forum, the default template will work, but it's not perfect. Let's also make some adjustments here:

```
tpl/forum.html
<{xoBlkTpl module="newbb" file="newbb_block.php" show_func="b_newbb_topic_show"
    options="time|5|0|2|1|0|0"}>
<table cellpadding="0" cellspacing="0" border="0">
  <{foreachq item=topic from=$block.topics}>
      <tr class="<{cycle values="even,odd"}>">
          <td><{$topic.seo_url}></td>
      </tr>
  <{/foreach}>
</table>
<p style="text-align: right;">
    <{$block.seo_top_allposts}> |
    <{$block.seo_top_allforums}>
</p>
<{/xoBlkTpl}>
```

Save it as *tpl/forum.html* and include it in your *theme.html* file. You're almost done: refresh your browser and see the results of your hard work (Figure 8-28)!

Finally, we need to edit the navigation panel and add the correct links:

```
<li><a href="<{xoAppUrl}>">Home</a>
</li>
<li><a href="<{xoAppUrl modules/publisher/category.php?categoryid=2}>">Travel</a>
</li>
<li><a href="<{xoAppUrl modules/publisher/category.php?categoryid=3}>">Digital</a>
</li>
<li><a href="<{xoAppUrl modules/publisher/category.php?categoryid=4}>">Food</a>
</li>
<li><a href="<{xoAppUrl modules/publisher/category.php?categoryid=5}>">Sports</a>
</li>
<li><a href="<{xoAppUrl modules/newbb}>">Forum</a></li>
```

Figure 8-28. Our home page now contains all the elements from our mock-up in Figure 8-3

This part of your code may vary, depending on your category ID.

And add something in the footer, such as copyright information:

```
<div class="content-general footer">Copyright 2011 my TinyMAG. All rights reserved.
    Powered by <a href="http://xoops.org/">XOOPS</a></div>
```

User Menu

The *login / register* link on the top right is static whether the user has signed in or not, which is not user-friendly. You might consider displaying a *logout / user* menu when the user signs in. You can use `<{if $xoops_isuser}>` to solve this:

```
theme.html (excerpt)
<{if $xoops_isuser}>
    <a href="<{xoAppUrl user.php?op=logout}>" class="header-login">Logout</a>
    <a href="<{xoAppUrl user.php}>" class="header-register">Profile</a>
<{else}>
    <a href="<{xoAppUrl user.php}>" class="header-login">Login</a>
    <a href="<{xoAppUrl register.php}>" class="header-register">Register</a>
<{/if}>
```

Publisher + Disqus

XOOPS's default comment system is quite old-fashioned (see Figure 8-29).

Figure 8-29. XOOPS's default comment system isn't very shiny

The user has to click the *Post Comment* button and then go to a new page in order to leave a comment. This is definitely not good for a start-up website: you want to encourage comments and communication. You could solve this by rewriting the comment system, but that would be a large project.

Instead, we'll use a simpler solution and make use of the Disqus service. Disqus (*http://disqus.com*) is a third-party service that provides powerful and modern commenting systems. We can integrate it into Publisher to replace the old commenting system.

However, it is not appropriate to use this integration in every situation. XOOPS has an integrated user system, so if you plan to build a community website, it's better to stick to the built-in system. However, in this case, the website is for a magazine and we don't need lots of community services. Thus the integration might be okay.

First you'll have to create an account in Disqus, and then register your website (see Figure 8-30).

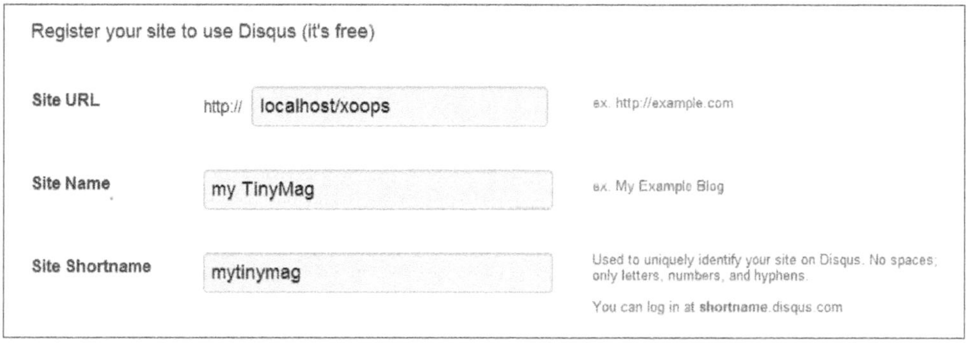

Figure 8-30. Create a Disqus account and then register your website

Then you'll have the option to change some settings and enable features, as shown in Figure 8-31.

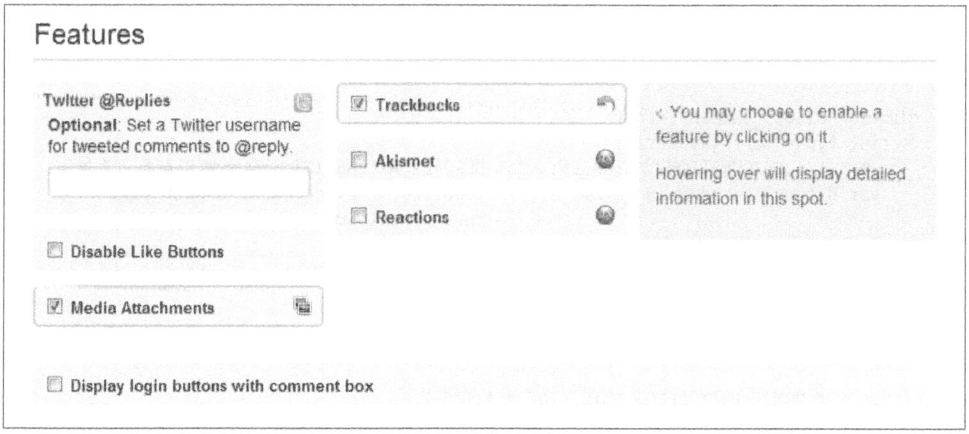

Figure 8-31. Disqus feature options at registration

After that, you will have to "install" the service. As you can see in Figure 8-32, there are many built-in platforms available. Unfortunately, we will have to install manually to integrate with Publisher. Click *Universal Code*.

Figure 8-32. Disqus offers many platform options, but for Publisher we need to do a manual install

First you will get a code snippet like this:

```
<div id="disqus_thread"></div>
<script type="text/javascript">
    /* * * CONFIGURATION VARIABLES: EDIT BEFORE PASTING INTO YOUR WEBPAGE * * */
    var disqus_shortname = 'example'; // required: replace example with your
                                      // forum shortname

    // The following are highly recommended additional parameters. Remove the slashes
    // in front to use.
    // var disqus_identifier = 'unique_dynamic_id_1234';
    // var disqus_url = 'http://example.com/permalink-to-page.html';

    /* * * DON'T EDIT BELOW THIS LINE * * */
    (function() {
        var dsq = document.createElement('script'); dsq.type = 'text/javascript';
            dsq.async = true;
        dsq.src = 'http://' + disqus_shortname + '.disqus.com/embed.js';
        (document.getElementsByTagName('head')[0] ||
            document.getElementsByTagName('body')[0]).appendChild(dsq);
    })();
</script>
<noscript>Please enable JavaScript to view the <a href="http://disqus.com/
    ?ref_noscript">comments powered by Disqus.</a></noscript>
<a href="http://disqus.com" class="dsq-brlink">blog comments powered by
    <span class="logo-disqus">Disqus</span></a>
```

After this step, you have two choices: the first is to use a module template override, and the second is to hack the module template directly. Because the latter approach can be used for other themes, it's the one I'll cover here.

Open */XOOPS/modules/publisher/templates/publisher_footer.html* (to find this file, you may have to analyze the template files and use your intuition):

```
publisher_footer.html
<{if $isAdmin == 1}>
    <div class="publisher_adminlinks">
        <{$publisher_adminpage}>
    </div>
<{/if}>
<{if ($commentatarticlelevel && $item.cancomment) || $com_rule <> 0}>
    <table border="0" width="100%" cellspacing="1" cellpadding="0" align="center">
        <tr>
            <td colspan="3" align="left">
                <div style="text-align: center; padding: 3px; margin:3px;">
                    <{$commentsnav}> <{$lang_notice}>
                </div>
                <div style="margin:3px; padding: 3px;">
                    <!-- start comments loop -->
                    <{if $comment_mode == "flat"}>
                        <{include file="db:system_
                        comments_flat.html"}>
                    <{elseif $comment_mode == "thread"}>
                        <{include file="db:system_comments_
                        thread.html"}>
                    <{elseif $comment_mode == "nest"}>
                        <{include file="db:system_
                        comments_nest.html"}>
                    <{/if}>
                    <!-- end comments loop -->
                </div>
            </td>
        </tr>
    </table>
<{/if}>
Publisher + Disqus | 97
<{if $rssfeed_link != ""}>
    <div id="publisher_rpublisher_feed">
        <{$rssfeed_link}>
    </div>
<{/if}>
<{include file='db:system_notification_select.html'}>
```

Replace the `<table>` structure with the code from Disqus:

```
publisher_footer.html
<{if $isAdmin == 1}>
<div class="publisher_adminlinks"><{$publisher_adminpage}></div><{/if}>

<{if ($commentatarticlelevel && $item.cancomment) || $com_rule <> 0}>
<div id="disqus_thread"></div>
<script type="text/javascript">
    /* * * CONFIGURATION VARIABLES: EDIT BEFORE PASTING INTO YOUR WEBPAGE * * */
    var disqus_shortname = 'mytinymag'; // required: replace example with your
                                        // forum shortname
```

```
// The following are highly recommended additional parameters. Remove the slashes
// in front to use.
// var disqus_identifier = 'unique_dynamic_id_1234';
// var disqus_url = 'http://example.com/permalink-to-page.html';

/* * * DON'T EDIT BELOW THIS LINE * * */
(function() {
    var dsq = document.createElement('script'); dsq.type = 'text/javascript';
        dsq.async = true;
    dsq.src = 'http://' + disqus_shortname + '.disqus.com/embed.js';
    (document.getElementsByTagName('head')[0] ||
        document.getElementsByTagName('body')[0]).appendChild(dsq);
})();
</script>
<noscript>Please enable JavaScript to view the <a href="http://disqus.com/
    ?ref_noscript">comments powered by Disqus.</a></noscript>
<a href="http://disqus.com" class="dsq-brlink">blog comments powered by
    <span class="logo-disqus">Disqus</span></a>
<{/if}>

<{if $rssfeed_link != ""}>
<div id="publisher_rpublisher_feed"><{$rssfeed_link}></div><{/if}>

<{include file='db:system_notification_select.html'}>
```

Remember to change *disqus_shortname* to your own shortname.

Then you'll have to replace the "comment count" of Publisher.

First, add the following code from Disqus to the *end* of *publisher_footer.html*:

```
<script type="text/javascript">
    /* * * CONFIGURATION VARIABLES: EDIT BEFORE PASTING INTO YOUR WEBPAGE * * */
    var disqus_shortname = 'mytinymag'; // required: replace example with your
                                        // forum shortname

    /* * * DON'T EDIT BELOW THIS LINE * * */
    (function () {
        var s = document.createElement('script'); s.async = true;
        s.type = 'text/javascript';
        s.src = 'http://' + disqus_shortname + '.disqus.com/count.js';
        (document.getElementsByTagName('HEAD')[0] ||
            document.getElementsByTagName('BODY')[0]).appendChild(s);
    }());
</script>
```

 Remember to replace the shortname here, too.

Then, add `#disqus_thread` after `<{$item.itemurl}>` in *publisher_item.html*:

```
publisher_item.html (excerpt)
<{if $display_comment_link && $item.cancomment}>
    <span style="float: left;">
        <a href="<{$item.itemurl}>#disqus_thread">
            <{$item.comments}> <{$smarty.const._MD_PUBLISHER_COMMENTS}>
        </a>
    </span>
<{else}>
    <span style="float: left;"> </span>
<{/if}>
```

Refresh your page, and you'll see the modern comment form is there, as in Figure 8-33!

Figure 8-33. Comment form built with Disqus

Please note that by default, Disqus will use a URL as an identifier to show comments. The best practice is to use a custom ID. This can be accomplished easily in Publisher—simply define those JavaScript variables in the first code snippet from Disqus:

```
publisher_footer.html (excerpt)
var disqus_shortname = 'mytinymag'; // required: replace example with your
                                    // forum shortname
var disqus_identifier = 'publisher-item-<{$itemid}>';
var disqus_url = '<{$item.itemurl}>';
var disqus_title = '<{$item.title}>';
```

And add:

```
data-disqus-identifier="publisher-item-<{$itemid}>"
```

to *publisher_html.html* as follows:

```
publisher_item.html (excerpt)
<{if $display_comment_link && $item.cancomment}>
    <span style="float: left;">
        <a href="<{$item.itemurl}>#disqus_thread"
        data-disqus-identifier="publisher-item-<{$itemid}>">
            <{$item.comments}>
            <{$smarty.const._MD_PUBLISHER_COMMENTS}>
        </a>
    </span>
<{else}>
    <span style="float: left;"> </span>
<{/if}>
```

I provide this integrated edition of Publisher for download in my code forge at *http://code.google.com/p/insraq/downloads/list* (see Figure 8-34).

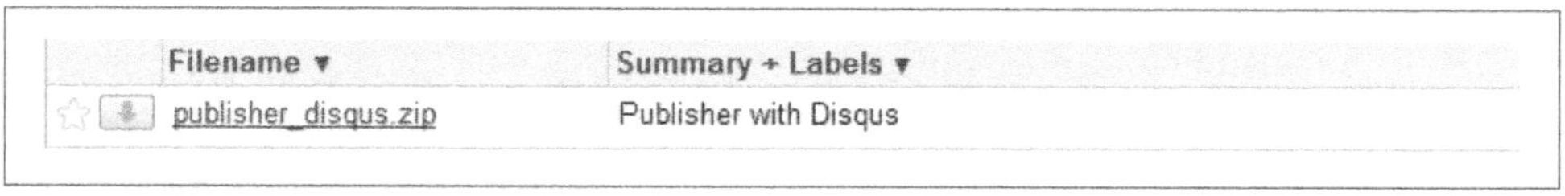

Filename ▼	Summary + Labels ▼
☆ ⬇ publisher_disqus.zip	Publisher with Disqus

Figure 8-34. An integrated edition of Publisher available for download

Final Check

The last thing to check before we make our website public is the permission settings. View the user website both as a normal user and as a visitor. Publisher has a permissions setting for each individual article; make sure you grant the corresponding user groups permission to view each article. The settings can be modified in the *Others* tab when you edit an article (see Figure 8-35).

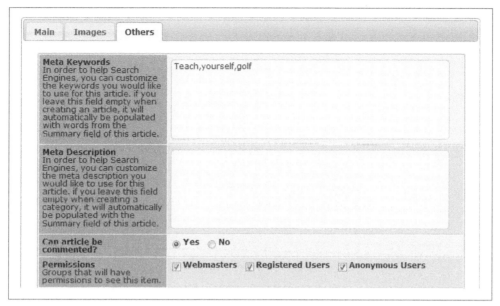

Meta Keywords In order to help Search Engines, you can customize the keywords you would like to use for this article. If you leave this field empty when creating an article, it will automatically be populated with words from the Summary field of this article.	Teach,yourself,golf
Meta Description In order to help Search Engines, you can customize the meta description you would like to use for this article. If you leave this field empty when creating a category, it will automatically be populated with the Summary field of this article.	
Can article be commented?	⦿ Yes ⦾ No
Permissions Groups that will have permissions to see this item.	☑ **Webmasters** ☑ **Registered Users** ☑ **Anonymous Users**

Figure 8-35. A permissions setting in the Others tab lets you set permissions for each individual article

 If you want to read through the detailed source code, or gain a fuller understanding of the code, you can get the source from *http://insraq.me/ files/book/mytinymag_ch8.zip*.

XOOPS Cheatsheets

XOOPS Resources

This appendix features handy tables and examples with XOOPS commands you will frequently use. A more detailed PDF, ideal for portability, is available on the book's website (*http://oreilly.com/catalog/9781449308964/*), as well as at *http://insraq.me/ book/*. Please report any bugs to me at ruoysun@gmail.com.

Table A-1. Header meta tags

Tag	Example output	Purpose
<{$xoops_charset}>	UTF-8	Output the character set
<{$xoops_langcode}>	en	Output content language
<{$xoops_meta_keywords}>	N/A	Output the meta keyword list
<{$xoops_meta_description}>	N/A	Output the meta description
<{$meta_copyright}>	N/A	Output the meta tag copyright
<{$meta_robots}>	index, follow	Output the W3C robot meta tag
<{$meta_rating}>	general	Output the meta tag rating

Table A-2. General XOOPS commands

Tag	Comment
<{$xoops_sitename}>	Site name
<{$xoops_slogan}>	Site slogan
<{$xoops_pagetitle}>	Current page title
<{$xoops_theme}>	Theme folder name
<{$xoops_url}>[a]	Site URL without the "/"
<{$xoops_banner}>	Site banner
<{$xoops_contents}>	Module contents
<{$xoops_footer}>	XOOPS footer

[a] This tag can be replaced by <{xoAppUrl}>, which basically achieves the same result.

Table A-3. User-related XOOPS commands

Tag	Comment
<{$xoops_isadmin}>	If the user is an admin?
<{$xoops_isuser}>	If the visitor is a user?
<{$xoops_userid}>	User ID (integer)
<{$xoops_uname}>	Username

Table A-4. XOOPS resource locators and links

Tag/code	Link
<{xoAppUrl backend.php}>	XOOPS/backend.php
<{xoImgUrl style.css}>	XOOPS/theme/yourtheme/style.css
<{xoImgUrl img/some.png}>	XOOPS/theme/yourtheme/img/some.png
<{xoImgUrl js/some.js}>	XOOPS/theme/yourtheme/img/some.png

More Resources

If you want to know more, here are some good online references:

- Smarty: *http://www.smarty.net*
- PHP: *http://www.php.net*
- XOOPS: *http://xoops.org*

About the Author

Sun Ruoyu is a UI designer, web designer, author, and XOOPS 3 core designer. He is a two-time XOOPS Innovation Award Winner (in 2009 for successfully leading the redesign project, and in 2010 for his contributions in improving UI and designs), and winner of the 2010 NEA OSS Forum "Best Technology" Award for XOOPS 3.

Colophon

The animal on the cover of *Designing for XOOPS* is a crested ibis (*Nipponia nippon*).

The cover image is from *Heck's Pictorial Archive of Nature and Science*. The cover font is Adobe ITC Garamond. The text font is Linotype Birka; the heading font is Adobe Myriad Condensed; and the code font is LucasFont's TheSansMonoCondensed.

Get even more for your money.

Join the O'Reilly Community, and register the O'Reilly books you own. It's free, and you'll get:

- $4.99 ebook upgrade offer
- 40% upgrade offer on O'Reilly print books
- Membership discounts on books and events
- Free lifetime updates to ebooks and videos
- Multiple ebook formats, DRM FREE
- Participation in the O'Reilly community
- Newsletters
- Account management
- 100% Satisfaction Guarantee

Signing up is easy:

1. Go to: oreilly.com/go/register
2. Create an O'Reilly login.
3. Provide your address.
4. Register your books.

Note: English-language books only

To order books online:
oreilly.com/store

For questions about products or an order:
orders@oreilly.com

To sign up to get topic-specific email announcements and/or news about upcoming books, conferences, special offers, and new technologies:
elists@oreilly.com

For technical questions about book content:
booktech@oreilly.com

To submit new book proposals to our editors:
proposals@oreilly.com

O'Reilly books are available in multiple DRM-free ebook formats. For more information:
oreilly.com/ebooks

O'REILLY®

Spreading the knowledge of innovators   oreilly.com

The information you need, when and where you need it.

With Safari Books Online, you can:

Access the contents of thousands of technology and business books

- Quickly search over 7000 books and certification guides
- Download whole books or chapters in PDF format, at no extra cost, to print or read on the go
- Copy and paste code
- Save up to 35% on O'Reilly print books
- **New!** Access mobile-friendly books directly from cell phones and mobile devices

Stay up-to-date on emerging topics before the books are published

- Get on-demand access to evolving manuscripts.
- Interact directly with authors of upcoming books

Explore thousands of hours of video on technology and design topics

- Learn from expert video tutorials
- Watch and replay recorded conference sessions

Spreading the knowledge of innovators   safari.oreilly.com

Lightning Source UK Ltd.
Milton Keynes UK
UKOW05f1053210316

270570UK00001B/64/P